2024

Anthology

A collection of creative works from the second annual
Rockaway Writers Rendezvous in Rockaway Beach, Oregon

ROCKAWAY WRITERS RENDEZVOUS 2024 ANTHOLOGY

Published by Rockaway Writers Rendezvous
Rockaway Beach, Oregon USA

2024 All rights reserved

This book may not be reproduced in whole or in part by any means without permission. For information: RWR Staff - info@RBWriters.com

The Rockaway Writers Rendezvous identity is a trademark owned by Rockaway Writers Rendezvous. For more information contact
RWR 9300 SOUTH PRAIRIE ROAD, TILLAMOOK, OR 97141 USA

Cover Photo 2024 Don Backman

Created by Team RWR:
Don Backman
Robin Bock
John Daily
Cosmo Jones
Kizzie Jones
Mary McGinnis
Neal C. Lemery
Robin Swain
Laura Swanson

1ST EDITION
April 2024

ISBN 979-8-9904812-0-6

Printed in the United States

www.rbwriters.com

For all creative writers everywhere, with love from Rockaway Beach

TABLE OF CONTENTS

Sponsors — 09

2024 Event Overview — 15

2024 Writing Competition — 31

Writing Competition Winners & Honorable Mentions

STUDENT ENTRIES
- 1ST PLACE - POETRY SEVENTEENTH SUMMER - MAUREEN DALY 39
- 2ND PLACE TIE - POETRY CURIOSITY 41
- 2ND PLACE TIE - POETRY KITCHEN 43
- 1ST PLACE - MUSIC LYRICS (UNTITLED) 44
- 1ST PLACE - FICTION ALWAYS 47
- 2ND PLACE - FICTION DROWNING 51
- 1ST PLACE - NONFICTION MY LIFELINE 53
- 1ST PLACE - JOURNALISM FREE COLLEGE AND WHY IT'S A SOLUTION 57

ADULT ENTRIES
Poetry
- 1ST PLACE A WISH IS JUST A WISH 65
- 2ND PLACE TIE HEART REASONS 67
- 2ND PLACE TIE PARTY DRESS 69

Honorable Mention
- A FLEETING MOMENT 71
- A PRAYER FOR HEALING 73
- COMMENT RATTRAPER UN COEUR 75

CONTRADICTION	77
HENRY JOSEPH	79
I AM	81
NEW POEM BASED ON POE AND PHANTOM OF THE OPERA	85

Fiction

1ST PLACE AD FINITUM ... 89
2ND PLACE RED SKY AT NIGHT, RUBY DELIGHT ... 93
3RD PLACE THE DAY OF THE PLAY ... 97

Honorable Mention

THE ADVENTURES OF BEGONIA HONEY DEEVINE	101
DIG UNDER WHERE?	105
LEAVING HOME	109
TIM	113

Nonfiction

1ST PLACE HOSTESS PIE ... 119
2ND PLACE THE PSYCHIC ... 123
3RD PLACE SINGLE GIRL ... 125

Honorable Mention

EL GALLO	129
I NEVER THOUGHT I WOULD…	133
IT'S ALL ABOUT THE CANINE	137
KINDERGARTEN GRADUATION MEMOIR	141
OF VALUE	145
PRAIRIE DOGS AND TUNNELS	147
SALMON CYCLE: ETHEREAL PASSAGE	151
TWO PANS	153
YAEKI-SAN	157

CONTENT WARNING: The subject matter of some stories contains topics, such as child abuse, death of child/parent, suicide, animal abuse, and sexual themes, that might not be suitable for some readers. We care about your mental well-being.

Need Support Now? *If you or someone you know is struggling or in crisis, help is available. Call or text or chat 988 or https://988lifeline.org/*

FOREWORD

The magic of writing and the mysterious journey it takes is on! It truly is the evolution of a writer's soul.

We build the characters from our hearts, experiences, and observations of the world around us, pouring our minds and souls into every word. Then, we stress about being technically correct, about being authentic, and about connecting with the reader. As the creative process begins, our subconscious prays that we do not run into the brick wall called writer's block!

Sitting in a coffee house with my friends, Cosmo Jones, Don Backman, and Neal Lemery, I told them, of all the scholarships I received, the only one I remember was the smallest one for $179. I received it by winning a poetry contest sponsored by a local writers' group. It wasn't the amount or the beaming faces of the ladies as they presented the check to me. It was Beth leaning in and saying, *"You're one of us now, you're a writer."*

I continued telling the guys, the recognition that I am a writer and a peer has helped me traverse many a brick wall. I wished we still had a writer's group here in town. We sipped on our coffees in silence, looking at each other. A few seconds later, we all said, *"Let's do it!"*... and that, my friends, is how the Rockaway Writers Rendezvous came to be!

Our dream is to inspire creativity and recognition for aspiring writers of all ages. We aim to raise scholarship funds for Neah-Kah-Nie High School students pursuing writing careers.

After much hard work from a generous volunteer team, we are pleased to present the first Rockaway Writers Rendezvous Anthology.

For the love of writing... Enjoy!

ROBIN SWAIN and TEAM RWR

THANK YOU TO OUR SPONSORS

FOUNDING SPONSORS

Investing in tomorrow.

TILLAMOOK COUNTY PARKS FOUNDATION

Without our volunteers and local support, this event wouldn't be possible. We would like to thank the Parks Foundation for being our founding sponsor and fiscal partner.

With their support we are able to collect donations and provide tax deductible donation receipts. In addition, their support reduces our overhead which means we can deliver more scholarships.

THE CITY OF ROCKAWAY BEACH

Thanks to a generous grant from our City, we have been able to offer a much more robust event this year. They have given us the ability to create a bigger foundation for years to come, and we are grateful that our town supports creativity and fosters community.

2024 MAJOR SPONSORS

Tillamook Estuaries Partnership

Grumpy's Cafe

Eugene Schmuck Foundation

Beach Break Vacation Rentals

Sasquatch Coffee Company

Oregon Writers Colony

Tie Breaker

The Lions Club

Rockaway Community Church

Tillamook County Pioneer

KTIL

StudioAtTheBeach.com

1888Press.com

Bock's Best

THANK YOU TO OUR PLATINUM ANTHOLOGY SPONSOR

NANCY ALBRO
ALL PROFESSIONALS REAL ESTATE

"As an experienced real estate agent, I offer you specialized knowledge for informed decisions. My unique market insight and negotiation skills will help secure the best price for your property, whether buying or selling. I offer valuable local tips and guidance in Portland West and North Oregon's coastal areas, ensuring a smooth decision-making process. In a tough market, my professional integrity guarantees your confidence in this significant life choice."

OFFICE
503-259-2100

CELL
503-703-8860

ALLPROFESSIONALSRE.COM

2024 EVENT PROGRAM

Friday, April 26 & Saturday April 27

Open Mic Performances

at Tie Breaker

Saturday, April 27

Workshops and Keynote Address

at Rockaway Community Church and the Lions Club

Sunday, April 28

Awards Breakfast and Networking

at the Lions Club

2024 EVENT OVERVIEW

KEYNOTE ADDRESS

The Healing Power of Stories
presented by Mark Yaconelli

In an increasingly fast-paced and fractured world, sharing stories can be a radical and deeply human practice for uncovering the ties that bind us to one another. Story invites us to step into the reality of another's existence and instead of judgment feel kinship. In the pages of Between the Listening and the Telling, storyteller, author, and activist Mark Yaconelli leads readers into an enchanting meditation on the power of storytelling in our individual and collective lives.

Find me online: markyaconelli.wordpress.com

ROCKAWAY WRITERS RENDEZVOUS 2024 ANTHOLOGY

WORKSHOP 1

Organizing and Maintaining a Helpful Writing/Critique Group

presented by Kizzie Jones

How do you find or create a writing/critique group that polishes your writing project while giving you a lift of confidence? In this session, you will learn the essentials of establishing group norms and creating a safe avenue for supportive and genuine feedback.

Find me online: kizziejones.com

WORKSHOP 2

So, You Want to Be a Writer?
presented by Randall Platt

A fun, creative, and interactive workshop for ages 12 and up (adults are welcome!) where mayhem often reigns, ideas are tossed about, challenged, honed, and within an hour, we will have plotted a novel, developed key characters, and created realistic motivations.

Find me online: plattbooks.com

WORKSHOP 3

Self Publishing Bootcamp
presented by John Daily

Ever dreamed of becoming a published author but didn't know where to start? Learn the essential steps to kick start your publishing journey!

Find me online: 1888press.com and j3mediafactory.com

WORKSHOP 4

Writing to Heal

presented by Sydney Elliott

Writing can be cathartic and healing, especially in nonfiction. But exploring past trauma via writing has pitfalls, not only for the writer but also the intended audience. This workshop will explore healthy approaches to the nonfiction narrative based on research, neuroscience, and the input of authors of various genres to create a tool kit for those wanting to discover the nature of trauma and its transformative powers.

Find me online: sydneyjelliott.com

Your writing will be informed by four cards dealt to you face-down from a deck that features lines of poetry by Lucille Clifton. You will start by turning over your first card, reading the line and beginning your poem. Then, at timed intervals, you will be asked to reveal each additional card as you write. This should inspire your work to take several unexpected turns. We all have unexpected lines in us that can move, surprise, and delight.

Find me online: pickpoetry.com

This workshop is for both fiction and nonfiction writers working on a manuscript they hope to submit for publication. The content will offer nuts-and-bolts tips on what readers will expect from your work and what agents and acquisition editors will be looking for in submissions. Lorincz will cover the basics with easy-to-apply suggestions ranging from developmental notes, editorial guidelines, and formatting requirements.

Find me online: literaryconsulting.com

ROCKAWAY WRITERS RENDEZVOUS 2024 ANTHOLOGY

WORKSHOP 7

Write for Film, Create Action Sequences

presented by Dawn Sellers

Writing good action for screenplays involves creating dynamic, engaging sequences that capture the audience's attention and drive the story forward. In this one-hour workshop, attendees will learn tips for writing effective action scenes using the "Show, Don't Tell" principle. By following this method, attendees will learn to write action scenes that are engaging, immersive, and effectively convey the story to the audience without using exposition as a storytelling tool.

Find me online: dawnsellers.com

Young adult fiction has never been bigger. How do we reach these teens? What issues are they interested in learning? What is this language they speak? What if I don't even begin to understand who and what they are in this day and age? These are not your grandparent's teens! They aren't even OUR teens! But they are teens and they are reading! Let's go find them!

Find me online: plattbooks.com

WORKSHOP 9

Ethical Use of A.I.
presented by John Daily

Artificial Intelligence is quickly changing the landscape of the publishing industry. Join this immersive 50-minute workshop and delve into the intricate world of Artificial Intelligence alongside fellow writers.

Find me online: 1888press.com and also j3mediafactory.com

In this workshop, a novice will learn how to format a play script and build a world in which their characters live.

Key elements include: What type of stage, their story is intended to be told on. Budget concerns. Story and character development, create conflict and resolution to end their play. Choosing the play type that fits the story they want to tell and making sure that there is a beginning, middle, and end. Create character and storyline arcs. Limit dialogue to only benefit the story being told. Proper layout. How to get your work performed.

How We'll Do It: Create a ten-minute outline as a group, creating the world, the characters, storyline, arcs, and ending. (If time permits dialogue as well).

Find me online: facebook.com/DougSellersWriter

ROCKAWAY WRITERS RENDEZVOUS 2024 ANTHOLOGY

Writing as a Creative Practice
presented by Isa De Quesada

In 1978, author Ray Bradbury told a group of aspiring writers to write a hell of a lot and that it didn't matter what the quality of the writing was, just sit in front of the typewriter and throw up every day. Yet, most writers struggle to sit in front of a blank page. To establish a "practice" that yields results is even harder to do. If this sounds familiar, then this workshop might be perfect for you.

Based on the journey of finding the motivation to get to the computer daily with ease and excitement to getting published, you will be introduced to materials and tools that can guide you on how to establish a daily sustainable writing practice and accomplishing solid revisions which will lead you to produce publishable pieces. The workshop will offer understanding of the submission process and how to implement it into your writing routine.

By the end of the workshop you will have explored the components to get you from blank page to publication and you will understand the Ten Plus One plus One Guide. The goal of this workshop is to empower you to walk away with a writing plan that utilizes creative play, focused revisions, and fits into your lifestyle.

Find me online: www.Editorforwriters.com

CATERING SPONSOR

Grumpy's
CAFE & BAKERY

Grumpy's has been part of Rockaway for decades and you can't miss it, their building is always decorated in creative and amazing ways that change throughout the season. Open for breakfast and lunch, they also bake lots of delicious goods and we are grateful to be able to share these with all Rendezvous attendees!

202 US-101, Rockaway Beach, OR 97136

ROCKAWAY WRITERS RENDEZVOUS 2024 ANTHOLOGY

RAFFLE SPONSOR

Tillamook Estuaries Partnership

HEALTHY WATERSHEDS FOR A THRIVING COMMUNITY

Based in Garabaldi, Tillamook Estuaries Partnership's dedication to the health and quality of local estuaries is built on the idea that communities rely on our waterways to thrive in commerce, recreation, and overall well-being — now and into the future

www.tbnep.org

ROCKAWAY WRITERS RENDEZVOUS 2024 ANTHOLOGY

OPEN MIC SPONSOR

Tie Breaker is a welcome new addition to Rockaway Beach. This sports themed restaurant and bar has worked hard to deliver a great experience to locals and travelers. We are grateful for their support this year so that we have a nice venue for our Open Mics!

194 US-101, Rockaway Beach, OR 97136

www.tiebreakeroregon.com

ROCKAWAY WRITERS RENDEZVOUS 2024 ANTHOLOGY

2024 WRITING COMPETITION

THE COMPETITION

This year we launched a creative writing competition. We created one for adults and one for students. The winners of both competitions are published in this very anthology! Student competition winners earn cash prizes as well. The purpose of this event is to raise money for scholarships to award to students pursuing further education in writing and communication.

THE JUDGES

Thank you so much to our judges! There were a lot of entries to read, and we are grateful to our volunteer judges for putting in the time to carefully consider every entry. We had a lot of professional experience on our judging panel, let's meet them!

Charles McNeilly

Charles is retired and has lived in Rockaway Beach since 2018 with wife Sue. Charles is currently Mayor of the City of Rockaway Beach. Sue and Charles raised their two children (Erin and Sam) in Beaverton, OR. Charles worked in banking, software development and electric utilities for over twenty years managing projects, products and processes. They are avid readers, enjoy attending plays, visiting with friends and family, and take multiple daily walks around town and on the beach with their border collie Abigail. Among Charles' favorite authors are Erik Larsen, Tony Hillerman and Louise Penny.

Mary McGinnis

My favorite thing as a writing and communication teacher was to sit beside students and watch them excitedly explore different ways of expressing themselves. I taught writing in high school and with community college and university for years, and I feel it enriched my life to work with so many writers. I am also a Rockaway Beach City Councilor. I joined the RWR as a judge (and full time volunteer) because I am thankful to see this group bring together our dynamic writers and promote an artistic cultural movement for Rockaway.

John Daily

John Daily has been writing and publishing books for over 15 years. Before moving to Oregon, he taught various technology, visual arts, and critical studies classes at LTU in Chatsworth, California, where he was eventually asked to help develop the university curriculum and serve on the Visual Arts Board.

John has been a technology consultant, actor, radio host, and founder of five small publishing companies including 1888 Press, J3 Media, Elysian Press, ATP (Alternative Travel Press), and UP (Unnecessary Press).

Laura Swanson

With over 40 years of experience, Laura Swanson describes herself as a "born reporter" with an intense curiosity about everything! Laura started her career here on the North Oregon Coast at a little newspaper called "The Fishrapper", learning all aspects of the business from an experienced newspaperman. Fast forward forty years, and she has amassed a wide range of knowledge and skills about nearly every type of media – and has written for national, regional and local publications.

Currently Laura is the Editor/partner for the online media resource the Tillamook County Pioneer - www.tillamookcountypioneer.net, providing news and information to the North Oregon Coast for a decade. The tenets of the Pioneer are truth, kindness and to benefit the community by providing the best, most accurate information to our readers.

WRITING COMPETITION WINNERS & HONORABLE MENTIONS

This is my favorite part! Lots of talent here!!!

STUDENT ENTRIES

"In the book of life, the answers aren't in the back."

Seventeenth Summer
Maureen Daly

by

Cheyenne Reeves

In "Seventeenth Summer," Maureen Daly's tale,
Of youth's awakening, where dreams set sail.
Amidst the pages, love's tender bloom, A journey through adolescence' room.

"In the book of life, the answers aren't in the back."
Words whispered softly, no courage to lack.
For Angie, the protagonist, unsure and shy,
Yet within her heart, passions do fly
"Sometimes you just have to turn around, give a little smile, throw the match, and burn all the bridges."
A call to adventure, to let go and flee, From comfort zones, to find destiny.
"Secrets, silent, stony sit in the dark palaces of both our hearts."
Hidden desires, within each soul's chest,
Longing to be free, longing to confess.
"Tonight, let's forget about looking ahead or behind."
In the magic of the moment, true joy we find,
Embracing the now, leaving cares behind,
In love's sweet dance, hearts fully entwined.
"With you, I'm happy."
Simple words, yet deeply true,
In love's embrace, skies forever blue. Seventeenth summer, a season to remember,
In the pages of youth, love's ember. So let us cherish, this coming of age,
In "Seventeenth Summer," on life's stage. With courage and love, we shall endure,
In the book of life, our stories pure.

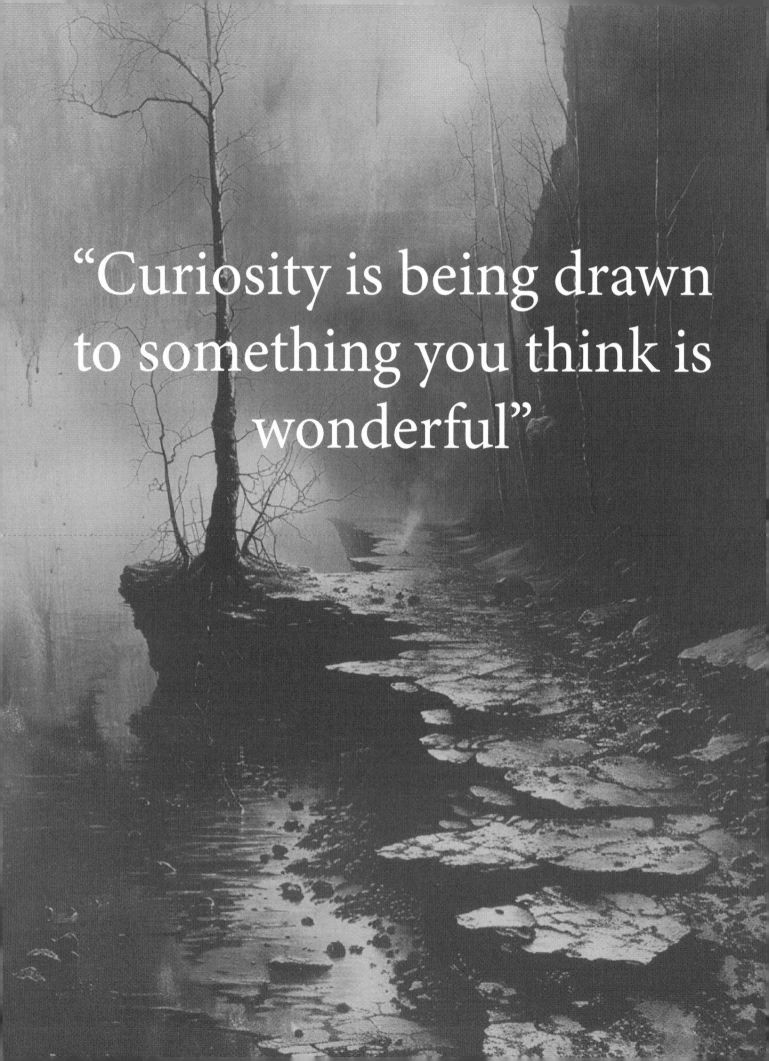

"Curiosity is being drawn to something you think is wonderful"

Curiosity

by

Trinity Charter

To me, it can be good, and bad.

Curiosity is venturing into the unknown, never knowing if you are to step onto solid ground, or a pit of disaster.

To me, curiosity is being drawn to something you think is wonderful, then getting hurt.

Stabbed even.

To me, it is blindness.

A feeling we lose ourselves in the midst of.

Curiosity is what it's called.

To me, it is divine.

To me, it is a disaster in disguise

"Her voice sounds like the melody of songs."

Kitchen

by
Tess Troxel

Jen, Jenny, Jennifer, mom.
Her voice sounds like the melody of songs.
Her hugs are warm and feel like home
Cardigans draped over my shoulders
I know I'm never alone
When she is nearby heat radiates from her joy
So warm and toasty, feels so homey.
I know I am so very lucky to have a mother who loves me
For she is a fierce Scorpio , so fun and loving
Puts others over herself not even caring
That she is not healthy she is not well
If her family is happy so Is she
For She'd jump in front of cars to save her daughters life
Not caring her child looks at her with spite
So overlooked, overrun
Her hair is messy fragile buns
Yet no matter what she feels or goes through
Her loving nature, and caring voice
Makes her priceless
For she is rare, nobody is like her or has her beautiful hair
Nobody can do what she can do
Nobody is as loving as my mother
Jen, Jenny, Jennifer, mom.
I love you more then anything
And I have always loved your songs

Music Lyrics

by

Marisa Walling

When I was a little girl

And I remember this like it was yesterday

I stood by my mother at the counter in the kitchen

And told her I would exceed her expectations of me

She said as a team your emotions overwhelm your state

You'll be lucky if you remember this date

The day you promised you would never hide just to seek

Make sure I don't lie

The truth I hold will thrive

And if you see me stray

Pull me back before your little girl goes away

Became unrecognizable

And I lost the person I was instantly

Put a bandage for a scrape on a gash

With bloodied hands

So I could open my curious mind

Now that she is older

She returns back to that place

The kitchen counter

Sees the past replaced

And turns to who she feels she left behind

A boy disguised as a man

I promised he would take her hand

Made poor little girls trust seeing as naive

Now she goes back to the counter drums a beat to this melody

She is tied down and only wants to be found

She is restrained and only wants to be saved

Make sure I don't lie

The truth I hold will thrive

and if you see me stray pull me back before your little girl goes away

If you see me stray pull me back before your little girl goes away

Make sure I don't lie

The truth I hold will thrive

And if you see me stray

Pull me back before your little girl goes away

If you see me straight, pull me back before your little girl goes

Always

by

Aislynn Thomas

My alarm clock goes off. I look at the clock and see the date. Today is the tenth anniversary of Ella's murder. I sit up and stretch. Once I'm mentally ready, I head to the bathroom so that I can take a shower. After I finished showing, I got dressed.

Then, heading back to my bedroom. I stopped by the photo of Ella. It was a photo of her at the beach. She is smiling, holding a small Lizard. Ella was missing two of her teeth; they had fallen out the week before. I remember her coming to school the day after it happened holding a five dollar bill, saying that the tooth fairy gave it to her. Her mother gave me the photo, saying it was her favorite of Ella. Her mother had it engraved Always, I feel tears welling in my eyes.

I don't want to cry, so I walk to my bed and lie down. I put on my headphones and play Ella's favorite song. "Walking on Sunshine" always puts me in a better mood. I decide to text my friends. Claire's name comes up first so I text her.

"Hey, C bear. How are you doing this morning? All I have been thinking about is what El would be like," I texted.

She didn't text back, so I figured she must be asleep. I then decided to text Mary and Betty. I got a quick text back from both of them.

My mother calls me downstairs. Her voice was urgent, so I jumped out of bed and quickly headed downstairs.

"Hey Mama, is something wrong?" I asked.

"Bea," chokes out my Mom.

She looks heartbroken. Her eyes are rimmed with silver tears, and she looks like she is going to start sobbing. I have only seen her this sad twice: when she told me about Ella and when she told me about Dad.

"Mommy, what is wrong?" I asked.

"Claire's mom just called me. She killed herself this morning," said Mom.

A sickening feeling takes over me. I no longer feel supported by my feet. I stumble onto my knees. My stomach is in a knot. My mom comes and tries to hug me but it just makes me feel sicker. So I shove her away from me. I can hear her talking but I can't make out what she is saying. My stomach is killing me. So I scream, trying to relieve the pain.

A week later, they hold Claire's funeral. Mary, Betty, and Claire's boyfriend, Al, sit next to me. Mary is holding my hand, too.

"I just can't believe this," said Mary.

Al and Betty all agree. After the funeral, everyone starts to talk about Claire.

Betty leaves early, not able to handle the sympathy anymore. Al drives her home. Mary and I stay. I stay next to Mary as she talks to people. Mary is the best at this—she always has been. Even when we were seven, she just knew how to expect people's sympathy. I shake hands with everyone Mary talks to.

The next couple of months, anyone who talked to the four of us always started with the words, "I'm so sorry for your loss." Al and Betty began hanging out a lot more. Learning on each other for support. I lean on Mary. I have always been closest to her.

After a week of dealing with this, people start to lean off of it. They stop saying sorry, and things go back to normal. It honestly feels so good. Right when things go back to normal, horror strikes again. Betty is killed. The original thought was that it was suicide. I don't know how I feel about that. I know that we were all sad about Claire, but I just don't see Betty killing herself. She was always so resilient.

The funeral goes the same as Claire's did. Al leaves early, and Mary and I stay together. Mary talks to everyone, and I stand next to her. My heart is just done. I don't think I can take anything else. It's just hurting me.

In four weeks, people go back to treating us the same, which feels good again. I don't want people to forget what happened to Betty and Claire, but every time I feel normal again, someone comes up to me and reminds me that my best friends are gone. Then I feel the pain all over again.

A week after, things go back to normal...then Al is found dead in a lake. The cops can't keep saying it's suicide after this. Three best friends were found dead, so back to back. They are still trying to find out what happened. Things don't go back to normal.

Everyone is scared of Mary and me. They are scared of us like they can't decide if we did it or if we are just super unlucky, like being friends with us will lead to their death. The other option isn't much better, and someone is trying to kill our whole group. Even with everyone in the school ignoring us, it's okay cause Mary and I have each other.

After a year, the cops still have no clue what happened. The last I heard, the cops were writing it off as a suicide pact. Friends just spaced it out so people wouldn't know. That doesn't make much sense to me, but I will move on. What can I do?

People move on, too. They start hanging out with Mary and me again. They stop feeling bad for us. They also aren't afraid of us or for us anymore. Everyone has moved on. I mean, Mary and I are still sad but are starting to feel okay.

My mother is working late tonight. So she isn't home yet. I see Mary climb through my window.

"Hey, Mary," I said.

"Hi, pretty girl. How are you today," asked Mary.

"I'm great," I said. I run over and hug Mary. I feel something go into me. I scream, and Mary does it again. I fall to the floor. Mary gets down on her knees and then sits on me. I feel the pain over and over again. I try to fight her off, but she is stranger than I am. Several minutes pass, and then she slowly gets off of my prone body.

"Why," I mumble.

"Ellie died, and everyone felt bad for us." a slight smile comes onto her face. "Then, people stopped caring," her brow furrowed. "Then Claire died, and people stopped caring even less... Then Betty and then Al..." The smile on her face growing as she says this.

"People just didn't care like they did when Ella died. I guess children dying is a lot sadder," said Mary. "Now you're dead, and people will feel bad again. I'll just have to find new friends," said Mary.

I stop moving.

She thinks I'm dead.

Mary then climbed out my window like nothing happened.

I do everything to stay awake. I stare at the clock... Trying to focus on something. All I can hear is my blood hitting the floor. It sounds like rain hitting the ground. A sound that would normally be calming to me, but every drop brings me closer to death. After a while, I come to the conclusion that I'm going to die. I return my focus to the clock, watching as it slowly changes.

My mom walks in about fifteen minutes after everything has happened. She screams. She runs over to me, sobbing. She starts trying to find a way to stop the bleeding, but there is too much blood from too many places. She can't figure out how to stop the bleeding. She is trying to talk to me, but I can only catch a word or two because she is crying so hard. The whole time she is doing this, I'm thinking about Ella, Betty, Claire, and Al. We are going to be together. Always.

My mom tells me she is going to grab something to stop the bleeding. I grab her arm to stop her from leaving me. I know that I can't hold on for too much longer, and I need her to know the truth.

"Mary did it," I force out, ignoring the pain. The last thing I hear before it goes dark is my mom saying my name, Beatrice...

"As I swim in a pool of my thoughts, I start to feel something..."

Drowning

by

Trinity Schenk Williams

As I swim in a pool of my thoughts, I start to feel something... something not normal, I can't breathe, can't swim, can't talk, all I can do is think. As I see the top of the water go farther and farther away, the more I go down, the more vivid my thoughts get. What if this happened? What if that happened, JUST STOP! I wake up in a bed but not just in any bed in a bed I'm not familiar with. There's wires, and a bunch of things hooked up to me. What's going on? I can't talk or move, I'm just laying, confused.... thinking... and still drowning.

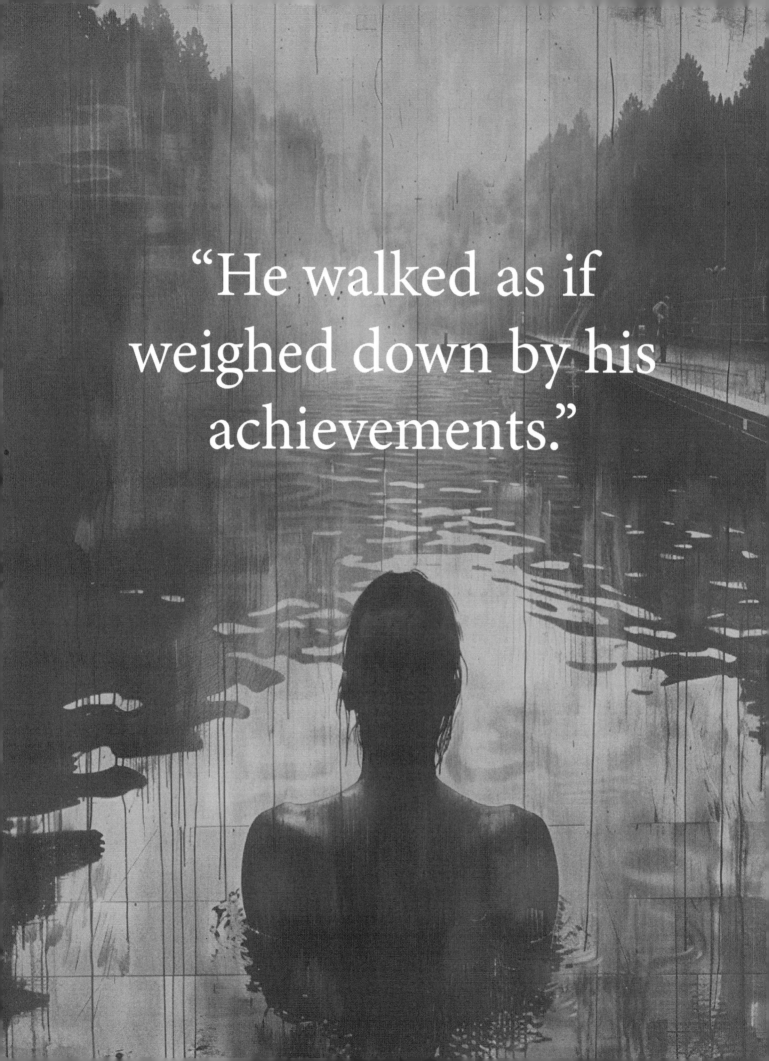

"He walked as if weighed down by his achievements."

My Lifeline

by

Alexandra Aguinaga

He walked as if weighed down by his achievements. Each medal dragged his posture down and by the tone in his voice it was clear that he wouldn't be satisfied until our neck was as heavy as his. The fluorescent lights added a green hue to the pool house that seemed to engulf everything. The water in my nose and his glare kept me from breathing easy. The smell of chlorine and other pool chemicals fogged over my thoughts, keeping me from thinking straight. By the look on his face it was clear that tonight was going to be a longer night than I had anticipated. With each instruction ordered I felt what was supposed to be an hour and a half practice stretch into three. Nothing I did was good enough tonight, but he wouldn't give up on me, "Again Alexandra!" his voice echoing through the pool house. The commanding tone that he often used would've stopped anyone dead in their tracks, if he hadn't been roaring like this all night. It was rare to hear him speak softly, not because he didn't know how but because no one ever spoke softly to him.

Coach Stefanos watched as I attempted what was supposed to be a back one and a half flip. Instead of landing head and hands first the water welcomed me face and stomach first. It hurt, it stung, I knew the pain was temporary but the embarrassment was forever as I half heartedly made my way back to the pool's edge. "What was that Alexandra?" he glared down at me.

"I dunno." I did know, it was a failure.

"Alexandra, listen to me, if you want to succeed in this sport you have to trust yourself, and if you can't do that then trust me" it was like he wanted to say it softly but instead his voice continued to boom across the pool, "Go up there and try again, this time I'll spot you" He walked over to the wall leaving me at the pool. Coach began to fiddle with some ropes attached to the wall that ran up to a pulley system at the top of the pool house. As he released the ropes from their hold on the wall a faded orange cone lowered from the ceiling to just above the diving board. I knew what he wanted me to do and I knew that I was too scared to do it.

The look on his face was impatient and told me to get a move on so I climbed out of the pool and slowly made my way up the diving board. I bounced on the edge, up and down, up and down, up and grabbed that barely orange cone and down. I messed with the cone for a bit, stalling as much as I could until the harness released it. Calling it a harness was too kind, it was a belt designed to dig under your ribs that Coach could use to lift you up during a dive. "Come on Alexandra, we don't have all day here" he urged. I secured the belt, letting it cut underneath my ribs, then backed up to the edge of the board until my heels were hanging off and the rest of my feet were trying to keep the balance that I so desperately lacked. I raise my hands so that they are perpendicular to the pool, and slowly begin to move the board as Coach begins to countdown, "Three, two, one, UP!" I jumped, throwing my hands backwards and propelling my legs over my head. Time slowed as I saw the water approaching, I was about to smack onto the unforgiving surface, I had under-rotated and now all I could do was brace myself. But the water never came, I felt the belt catch underneath my ribs suspending me in the air. Coach was holding onto the rope keeping me in the air, "Alexandra, I know you can make it all the way around but you don't seem to know that, trust your-" I assume he was saying "yourself" but he had already let go of the rope dropping me into the water.

I want to stay underwater and I am heavily considering just sinking to the bottom when I feel him tugging on the belt. So I let myself float up to the surface, swim back to the edge, climb out and up to the diving board. I again back myself up to the edge of the board and he once again begins his countdown. As he yells "UP!" I spring off the board throwing my arms and legs even harder this time and I feel him pull up on the rope giving me more air time to complete my rotation before plunging back into the water, it was nowhere close to a perfect dive but at least this time it didn't hurt. "Again Alexandra! Until you trust yourself" he almost had a hint of excitement, in his voice. So I made my way to the edge of the board, my heels a little farther back and my feet a little more steady.

I counted with him this time "Three, two, one, Up!" I threw my legs, my arms, my whole body up and backwards. Time slowed like I was suspended in the air but this time I was flying through it, one flip and then the half, I saw the water for a moment before entering hands then head, body then legs. I let myself stay underwater and take in the fact that I actually completed the dive. Completed it well even. "Alexandra!" My name was garbled by the water so I swam up to the surface.

"Yeah?"

"I didn't help you at all," he stated. I noticed that the rope was hanging behind him "I told you to trust yourself, that is all you need in this life"

By the time diving exited my life I just about hated Coach Stefanos. He was a hardass that pushed me and my teammates to our limits. He broke his players down to rebuild them into carbon copies of himself. I hated him because he added a challenge to my life that I lacked. I hated him because he wouldn't let me get away with giving anything less than my all. Until that point in my life there had been no one that truly pushed me. No one that had let me fail in order to succeed.

"What can be done to advance forward?"

Free College and Why It's a Solution

by

Kewi Carver

In any well functioning society, there is always one essential question that needs to be asked to keep things afloat: What can be done to advance forward? Of course, because humans are human, everyone has different ideas of what that should look like. It can be extraordinarily difficult to know what the next step should be. Fortunately, there is an answer. Many experts and citizens alike agree that a free college system would be a smart and realistic implementation for any America to make. There are many doubts that come along with the idea of free college, but the benefits of increased access to education, economic growth, and the weight it would take off current and future students would far outweigh the negative.

One of the number one reasons that people do not attend college is the cost. Too many students colleges are set up like a country club, where only the rich and privileged get a chance at a high paying job and livable wage. According to dropout statistics recorded by Dr. Imed Bouchrika, 51% of all college dropouts are due to expenses. Many of these dropouts are bright students, but because of the sheer cost of education, many people who come from low income families even with scholarships will not be able to attend college and finish it. Making college free will wipe out this barrier and open more opportunities to people to receive the education they deserve. According to the VCU Center On Society and Health, "Adults with more education tend to experience less economic hardship, attain greater job prestige, develop a higher social rank, and enjoy greater resources that contribute to better health." (Virginia 2015) This information helps us achieve a more developed understanding of the fact that a higher level education is not only essential to getting many jobs, but also for quality of life. Studies have shown that people with a higher level of education on average live longer lives.

Something else that must be taken into account is the current cost of living. The average cost of living per month in the US is $2,500 to $3,500 per month. For perspective, the majority of college students are in their late teens to early twenties, working a part time of full time fast food job. According to data from the Bureau of Labor Statistics, the average fast food employee only makes $27,000 a year. It is completely unrealistic to expect somebody barely out of high school to pay off student loans in the tens to hundreds of thousands of dollars if they can barely even afford to live. Implementing free college would give young struggling adults the ability to use their money to survive instead of making the rich even richer. If students are able to afford their clothing, food housing, bills, and don't have debts to pay off, they are much more likely to finish college. Finishing college has been shown to make people more independent, have a higher level of confidence, and have more interpersonal skills.

Finally, the amount of economic growth that free college would bring is astonishing. Having more educated people with healthier, happier lives means more people in high demand jobs. With college debts no longer holding people back, massive numbers of great minds begin flocking into high paying fields that they are desperately needed in. The more people working in these jobs, the more money society rakes in as a whole. A common claim regarding free college is that it isn't worth it to the general public because of how much it would raise our taxes. However, according to The Department of Education, "A tuition free program would yield a total of 371.4 billion in additional federal and state tax revenue, along with private after tax earnings gains of 866.7 billion in the first 11 years. By the end of this period, the additional annual tax revenue would exceed the program's annual cost – higher education not only provides a path for economic self sufficiency, it also contributes to positive outcomes such as improved health, reduced crime, and a greater sense of well being." (Eric 2020) This shows that even though yes, the cost will be high, more money is made than lost. It's exponential growth.

Another claim that is often made is why should we have free college if not other countries are doing it? The thing is, other countries are doing it. There are many other countries with successful free college programs, with citizens regularly utilizing their free education. Germany, France, and Norway are just a few of the many well known countries that have successful free education programs. Free college is not some new revolutionary idea that has never been done before. As of right now, America has the highest tuition fees in the world, and there is absolutely zero reason that this is necessary when its citizens could be enjoying the benefits of free education. America wouldn't be the first country to have free college, and it cannot be the last.

Taking all of this into account, it is clear that America should have a free college education system. By implementing free college it would not only grow the economy, but it would also increase the level of education given to the general population, and provide relief to current and future generations that wish to go to college and pursue a meaningful career. All of these things are incredibly important because it would improve people's health, reduce crime rate exponentially, and would increase the quality of life of all American citizens. As a society, it's time to take a step in the right direction, and implement free college into the system, for the betterment of communities, the country, and the world.

Works Cited:

Virginia Commonwealth University: *"Why Education Matters to Health: Exploring the Causes."*

Societyhealth.vcu.edu, Center on Society and Health, 13 Feb. 2015

Societyhealth.vcu.edu/work/the-projects/why-education-matters-to-health-exploring-the-causes.html#gsc.tab=0

Fast Food and Counter Workers. (2023, April 25). www.bls.gov

https://www.bls.gov/oes/current/oes353023.htm

Carnevale, A., Sablan, J., Gulish, A., Quinn, M., & Cinquegrani, G. (2020). THE DOLLARS AND SENSE OF FREE COLLEGE EXECUTIVE SUMMARY.

https://files.eric.ed.gov/fulltext/ED608988.pdf

Bouchrika, Imed. *"College Dropout Rates: 2022 Statistics by Race, Gender & Income."*

Research.com, 22 Aug. 2022, College Dropout Rates: 2024 Statistics by Race, Gender & Income | Research.com

ADULT ENTRIES

POETRY

A Wish is Just a Wish

by

Jennifer Cloer

I wish.

I wish that together we could have explored the history of brain disease and psychosis, madness and lunacy, learned from those who came before and slayed the demons in your mind.

I wish that could've cured you.

I wish it had been less about her, less about them. I wish our conversations could've been about art and about science and about the wonders that reflect back to us from the moon above.

I wish we would've laughed more and drank less.

I wish we would have taken the fight beyond the tired clinics, the sad psychiatrists and sorry social workers. And then found peace in the fields and the oceans and the trails and the rivers.

I wish I could've saved you again. And again and again. From him, from them. From the stranger you went home with and then stayed with until you called me to come get you.

I wish you could have known the depths of my sorrow and the depths of my love. I wish we'd had more time.

I wish.

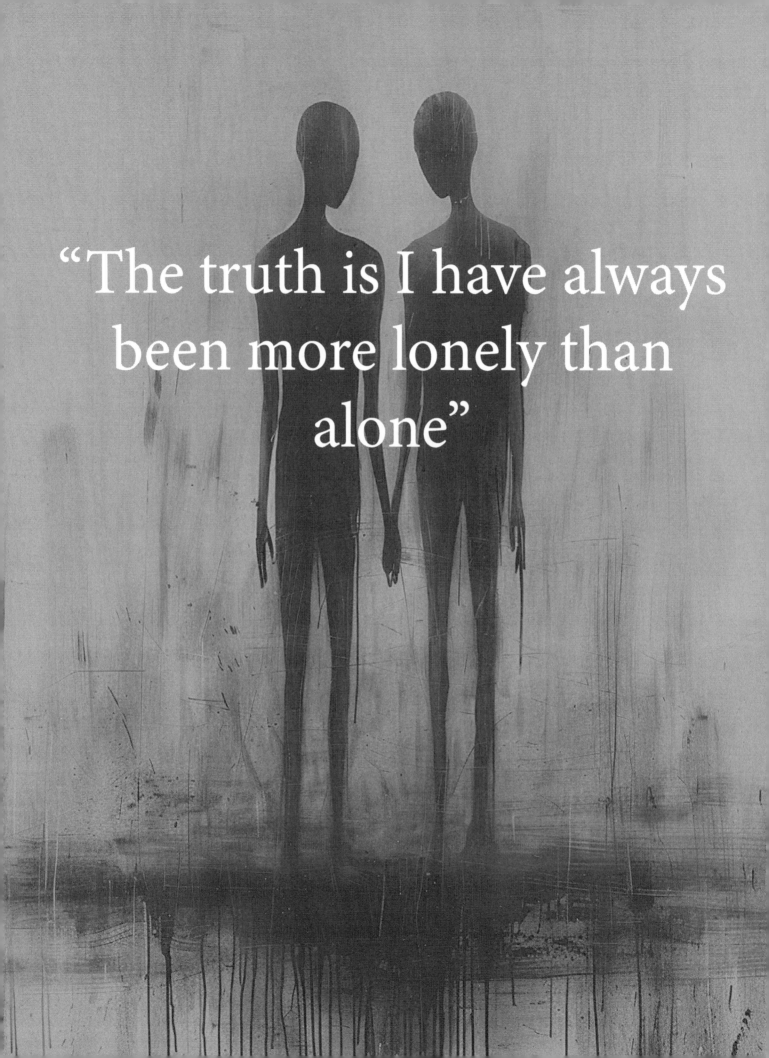

Heart Reasons

by

Jack Beisel

I have not been sleeping,
In the morning I don't seem to care
I am still alive, but please forget me,
If in your mind, you find me there

I will follow and surrender
To the man I have become at last
Want to go back to where no one had a future, and no one had a past

I left in a hurry, you left on your own
My prayers were left unanswered
Like my voice couldn't reach "the throne"
The truth is I have always been more lonely than alone
And the heart has its reasons, that reason will never know

Met a songbird in the winter, in this land of broken trees
It has always been a sweet song, that could bring me to my knees
Was I a martyr or a liar? Sometimes I just can't tell
I'll admit I tried to claim your heart, as the sword on which I fell

You only love me when you're drunk
Only kiss me when we're alone
Only hold me when your lonely
And miss me when you're low

The truth is I have always been more lonely than alone
And the heart has its reasons
Reason never knows

If I convince myself to stay here,
Will I lead or will I be led?
I am not and never was,
Another wound from which you bled

Another outline to a story,
That was better left unsaid
Just another keepsake,
And ghost that haunts your bed

You told me not to speak with you,
So I can't say these things
In this house that's always quiet,
In a city that never rains
And you can go back to your old boys,
They all know the way you taste
One thing we have in common,
We make the same mistakes

There are heavens I have been to
Hell is right with us tonight
If your love is not the one to save me,
Mine will have to be alright

The truth is I have always been more lonely than alone
And the heart has its reasons
Reason never knows

Party Dress

by

Shannon Perry

In the spring

the cedar tree

puts on her party dress.

Ferns make the ruffles

around the hem.

Green velvet overlaid

on brown brocade

and silky fronds adorn

her lithe form.

Her feet sparkle with dew

like silver slippers.

Branches form her long flowing hair

and the play of sunlight flatters her.

She holds hands with her sisters

and steps gracefully

among the tiger lilies

and bleeding hearts

The waltz toward summer has begun.

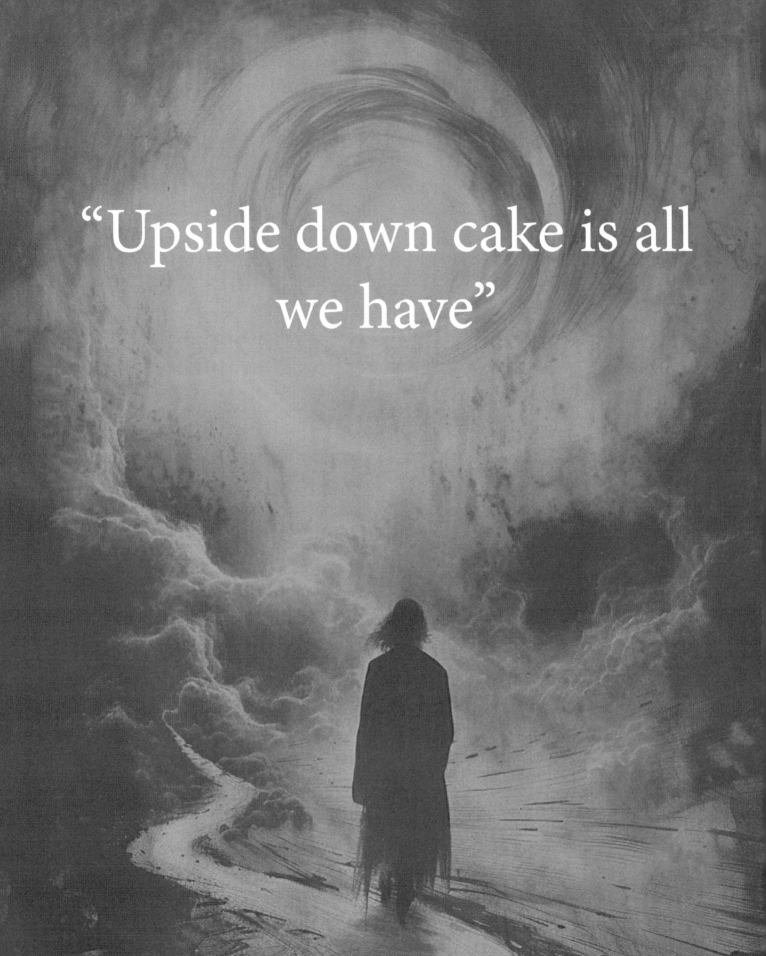

> HONORABLE MENTION
> Poetry
> Adult Competition

A Fleeting Moment

by

Amber M. Handel

Dig deep and fly high middle of the road
Like a tight rope all in disguise
No left no right just dust in the way
Nothing to adhere to nothing to try
Keep moving forward without shame or blame
Upside down cake is all we have
Backwards and sideways in between
A good dream a bad dream
Much of what it seems
Go up go down stay where you are
Is all that it means

"What do we do with all this hurt?"

ROCKAWAY WRITERS RENDEZVOUS 2024 ANTHOLOGY

**HONORABLE MENTION
Poetry
Adult Competition**

A Prayer for Healing

by

Sherri Levine

for Annie

How do you say goodbye to someone

who has hurt you?

How do you say goodbye in the room

where your mother lies in a hospice bed

and stares at the ceiling?

Is it heaven, this transition?

Blue swollen feet, metallic wafting skin.

Did Annie really want to say you, "You fucker."

Instead, she sang the Shemah on Zoom

every night for a week

while the caregiver flipped through

the newspaper, baked bread, swept the floor.

How do you say goodbye to someone who has hurt you?

The wooden spoon, tearing the shirt, shrieking?

To understand I sought out a rabbi's wife,

a death doula who charged a fortune.

At night, I swam at the Y's swimming pool,

each stroke, each stretch

a letting go of my own pain.

What do we do with all this hurt?

How did my Annie say goodbye?

I remember when she

wheeled my mother outside

for fresh air, sun on her neck,

when she held her limp hand,

whispered in her ear;

my mother's head drooped

like an unhardened clay puppet.

Did she say I love you?

Did she say I forgive you?

I wish I could have been a hummingbird,

hovering above the balcony

sipping on sugar.

my small heart beating,

fluttering my little wings

buzzing through.

Comment Rattraper Un Coeur

by

Karen Keltz

First, when you address the heart,
Call it "Sweetheart," "Dearest,"

Or even, "Mon Coeur,"

But even better

Show it what you mean.

Hold it when it's sad

Pat it on the back

And say, "There, there,

It will be all right,"

So it knows you can love

Its ugly crying face.

Bring it freshly baked

Chocolate chip cookies in bed

Or hot chocolate with whipped cream.

Write a poem with it as your subject.

Take it dancing because the heart

Makes you feel like dancing

For no reason.

Every day do one selfless thing

To make its life easier—

Take out the garbage.

Do the dishes.

Change a diaper.

Pick up a baby bird and return it to the nest.

Say, "This dinner is delicious!"

Look into its eyes

And say,

"You make me feel like

the luckiest person alive."

Pay attention, listen,

And say, "Oh, how I love you!"

Every day.

That's how you catch

And keep

A heart.

Contradiction

by

Jessy Frieze

Gruesome cracks across my back
reaching into those pools of deception

deeply inwards pushing to outerworlds
and underworlds I've found myself

the map only discovered through trauma
with no place to seek its refuge in resilience

My chest puffed with golden infamy
lost only to the broken mirror I can't see
Can I simply get lost forever in the fun house?

Temptation in my own self degradation
Finally I rejoice in my comforting despair

Shadows have illuminated my fat skeleton
forever alone in sweet healing community

Please don't be on fire like you were in April

Inspiration strikes only to the idle hands
Mist up the bifocals so the vision opens

Take me for what I am without meaning

Hope is found during hide and seek exercises
I'll understand when the message obscures

Symbolism and synchronicity in Cyrillic script

The woods are dark and deep inside the cabin
I will empty the shelves to ship them away

No time for play, there is work to be done

Once I begin

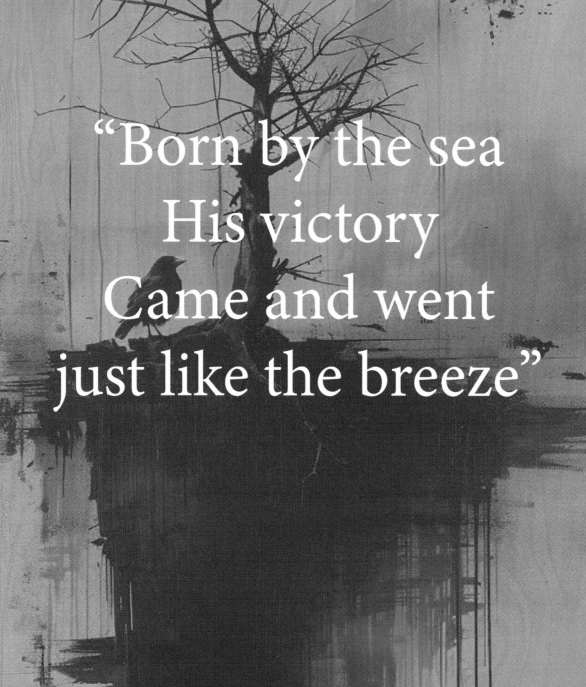

"Born by the sea
His victory
Came and went
just like the breeze"

HENRY JOSEPH

by

Eric Sappington

Born Foley Creek, crooked trees

Henry Joseph Hurricane

Came into this life

Knowing just what to do

Mama's pride,

Father stride,

Brother, who never left his side

Now he flies the sea

With an eagle's view

Now mama cries

Daddy rides

Baby sleeps by fireside

That Henry Joseph

Knows just what to do

Born by the sea

His victory

Came and went just like the breeze

Now he's like a dream

Beyond on the coast

Before you came around
It was quiet around here
Before you came around this town
Before you came around
It was quiet around here
And then you went out
Without a sound

Summertime, the hills we climb
Searching for the golden find
Laugh away the days
And the common blues
Your lover's near
You hold her dear
Protect from her greatest fear
That one day
You will be the one she'll lose

A momentary lapse
Of reason if you will
The shine has simply lost its glow
Born by the sea, his victory
Came and went just like the breeze
Now he's like a dream beyond the coast.

Before you came around
It was quiet around here
Before you came around this town Before you came around
It was quiet around here
Then you went out
Without a sound.

I Am

by

Jazzy Mitchell

Your eyes compel me

Although I dare not look—

Like Pallas, they reflect an unfathomable wisdom.

Your smell is comforting

Although I must turn away—

Your sweetness clears and befuddles my mind with one inhalation.

Your voice is like honey

sliding over my soul—

Although I miss many of your words while staring at smiling lips.

Your touch pierces my defenses

So that I tense—

Fearing my body's blatant reactions.

I taste your spirit—

It is never enough.

I continually thirst to know all that is you.

Frustration prevails.

Wanting more

Demanding nothing

Indicating nothing

I am nothing.

I am the dog on too short a leash
To reach the succulent bone.
I am Damocles threatened by the sword—

No, worse, I am not even allowed to sit at the feast.
I am the lead batter who breaks a leg
Before the state championships.
I am the knight in the locked tower
Looking out the window at his love in the garden,
Unable to converse, touch, or look
Into his beloved's eyes.
I am bereft, denied,
I am in love.

Fear prevails.
Wanting more
Demanding nothing
Indicating nothing
I am nothing.
I am the deepest, darkest secret
I dare not admit.
I am alone on the raft
On the wide-open ocean.

I am the speaker at the podium
Without the speech.
I am the freshman
In the new school.
I am afraid, unprepared,
I am in love.

Vulnerability prevails.
Wanting more
Demanding nothing
Indicating nothing
I am nothing.
I am the naked babe
Before the wolf.
I am the person who pushes you out of the car's path,
Now taking your place.
I am the one who looks unflinchingly into your eyes,
Allowing you to see my soul.
I am before you now, head bowed,
Awaiting your judgment.
I am revealed, waiting,
I am in love.

"Do you hear the hidden music?"

New Poem Based on Poe and Phantom of the Opera

by

Valerie Bohnke

The pendulum sways to the dark

Eternal closeness, nearness

Side to side, beat to beat

Where is the phantom?

Do you hear the hidden music?

Do you see the pain?

His heart beating, burning behind his mask?

Close your eyes

Can you feel the blood in the veins of the night?

Stillness pulsates memories

Do you remember?

Her touch? Her look? Shadows, only shadows

The music is quieter, so quiet, a faint whisper

Circling above gravestones

Only she can hear tears fall upon his face

FICTION

"Dinner always on time. Let me sleep on his bed. Took my side in any dispute with the cat. He lays it on thick. He always was an over-the-top kind of character."

Ad finitum

by

Justin Roberts

I am sure the end is nearly here. I do not know how I know, because I have never been here before. But somehow I know.

My beloved wife, Alice, comes into the room. "I have contacted Malcolm and Mary. They will be coming to visit us today."

"It will be great to see them again. Such great kids."

She fluffs up my pillow. It seems a long time now since I have left my bed. "Where is Corky? He usually lies on my feet."

She does not reply for a while. "He died last month, remember. We buried him in the back yard."

"Now I remember." But I don't. "Such a good dog. We had such great times together."

She nods in agreement.

I must have drifted off again.

When I wake up again, Mary is standing next to my bed. "Hi, dad." She kisses me on the cheek.

"Thanks for coming. Good to see you. Are David and the kids with you?"

"No, we felt it best for the kids not to come. David stayed with them."

"Yes. Best not to interrupt their studies."

I drift off again.

When I wake up again, Alice is holding my hand. No one else is in the room. "Was Mary here?"

"Yes."

"Where is she now?"

"She has gone to the airport to pick up Malcolm and Judy."

"Where is Corky?"

The answer is slower in coming this time. "He is outside, but don't worry. I know exactly where he is."

I drift off again.

When I wake up again, the whole family is standing around my bed. Malcolm holds one hand and Judy the other. "Great to see you. Thanks for coming." Alice sits down by my head and strokes my forehead. Mary is hugging her.

When I drift off again it feels different. I seem to be drifting in space. I can look down and see my body. Alice is crying and she is being held by the kids. I want to say 'Please don't be sad, I love you' but I cannot form words anymore.

I keep drifting towards an intense bright light. Am I falling or is it that the light is coming closer? I am overwhelmed by the light, I am disoriented and confused, and then suddenly I seem to arrive in a different kind of realm. I make out two presences. They do not have any definite form, but somehow they seem familiar. One of them speaks, not in words but in thoughts. "Welcome son. We have come to guide you." Recognition dawns. These are my parents.

"It is wonderful to see you again. I guess we will now be a family for all eternity."

"Actually it is not quite that simple."

"No?"

"We will be returning to the Universal Spirit, and take you along with us."

"So we will be together."

"Yes and no. You see when we merge with the Universal Spirit we lose our identities, including our memories. So once we all are at one with the Spirit we have no individual identity."

"But right now you do seem to have an identity and a memory."

"Yes. When we are tasked with a mission, such as welcoming you, our memories are temporarily restored."

"I see. So other than these missions, do we reside permanently in the Spirit?"

"Only until we are returned to earth as a new life form. In other words until we are reincarnated."

"And how often does that occur?"

"There is no set time. It can be days, or even centuries."

"What are we reincarnated as?"

"That depends on the kind of life you lived. If it was a good one, it will be as a higher form of life. If it was a bad one, you might need to start all over again as a low form of life."

"Have either of you ever been back?" My mother shakes her head, but my father says, "Yes once. But I was not there for very long." He doesn't say what he went back as and I decide not to ask.

My mother continues, "There was a strange case not so long ago. Someone got sent back immediately. Didn't even get to be part of the Universal Spirit."

"Yes, I heard something along those lines. The Spirit refused to have him. His name was Trump, or something like that. You didn't happen to know him did you?"

How should I answer this one? Clearly what happens on earth are not widely known in the Spirit world. Should I try to tell them everything I know? Perhaps not. In the end I simply say, "No. I have never met him." It is close enough to the truth. I then add, "Do you know what happened to him when he went back?"

"No. Not a clue. I did hear he was sent back as a cockroach. He must have done some truly terrible things." If this is a question I choose to ignore it. This is not the time to talk about the suffering and ruin he wrought upon the country. In some ways I am glad to be away from his legacy. Instead I simply say, "You are probably right."

"Enough talk for now. We can catch up later. We need to take you to the Presence who will decide on your next reincarnation, whenever that occurs. We will wait here. When you are through we will escort you to your merging with the Universal Spirit."

I now seem to be in some kind of nebulous chamber. It is dominated by an imposing presence whose form I cannot make out. It is not exactly human or anything familiar. It speaks, not words but thoughts. "I have gone through your history. You seem to have led a reasonably good and productive life."

I am not sure if I am supposed to respond to this, so I say nothing.

"And you did at least make some really smart choices."

"Do you have any of them in mind?"

"Yes. You married Alice. Very smart choice."

I decide not to ask any more questions. Quit while ahead seems the smart thing to do.

"Well, on reincarnation you are on the border line of being promoted to the next higher form of life. Let's hear from a witness. It might sway your case one way or the other."

A new form materializes. I cannot make out what it is, but somehow it seems familiar. As it begins to talk, I suddenly realize who it is. It is Corky.

Corky tells the Presence what a good person I had been. Plenty of walks on the beach. Lots of treats. Dinner always on time. Let me sleep on his bed. Took my side in any dispute with the cat. He lays it on thick. He always was an over-the-top kind of character.

In the end the Presence says, "Enough. I have made up my mind. You will be reincarnated as the highest life form possible. You will go back as a dog."

I can see the Presence more clearly now. As he smiles, he reveals his canine teeth.

Corky and I leave to join my parents, and all of us together merge with the Universal Spirit.

Red Sky at Night, Ruby Delight

by

Tessa Floreano

"Come along, my dears. We'll make camp below."

Amid the lush green forest of the Western Ghats, Laila the night shepherdess expertly drove her sure-footed goats down the steep mountain path to the river. Under a crimson moon and maroon clouds, she dallied, and imagined grabbing a net and the tallest ladder to snag rubies from the sky. Sighing, she ceded defeat to her treasure hunting fantasy. It was a poor substitute, but the only treasure she knew she could be sure to get for herself was to snag a trout out of the Cauvery River to roast for her Christmas breakfast.

Lately, her day sleeps had been short and full of strange dreams of a cloaked man, longing eyes, and a thick accent she did not recognize. She yawned and shook her head to clear it. A quiet moment reading the lyrical poems of Lalleshwari was exactly what Laila craved, and she promised herself time with the precious book after dinner. The words of the medieval Kashmiri mystic never failed to still the loneliness of her herdswoman's heart.

Laila was the last of her kind and no man had ever wanted this life with her. Too remote, many had said. Too wild, said another. And thus, as the years passed, she resigned herself to being alone in the world.

Skirting the Madikeri foothills, Laila and her flock arrived at the water's edge. She corralled her charges under a grand canopy of rudraksha trees.

"Follow your dreams because they always know the way forward."

"All right, settle down." She shushed their bleating with a tap of her hook on their rumps. "It is Christmas Eve and I have a feast to prepare." She swallowed a lump in her throat, wishing she had some fanciful gift to open, but she brushed away such foolishness.

After a quick meal of roti, tiger fish, and fried mango, she threw wood on the dying embers and stretched out in front of her small wintertime fire. In one hand, she held her precious verses, and in the other, a soothing tea of Tulsi and rose petals—a Christmastime ritual she had observed since her orphaned childhood.

"Ahhh, magical," she said aloud, kissing her book and laughing. "The only thing missing . . ."

". . . is chocolate," a man interrupted, his head poking out of a tree across the river, "for you deserve a magical treat this festive season."

Laila sat up. She dropped her book and set down her tea. In a flash, she got up and pulled out her kukri. She pointed the knife at the unexpected man. "I am Laila of the Night. Who are you?"

The man from her recurring dream parted mahua branches and walked out of the thicket. He stood facing her with palms up and no weapon visible. Slowly, from inside his colorful cloak, he extracted a beautifully wrapped bundle, then bowed.

"I am Mincaye, a shepherd from Ecuador. I sold my flock and my land to travel here. You enchanted me in my dreams, and I felt called to find the last of the night shepherdesses."

A warmth surged through her heart remembering her late father's advice:

Follow your dreams because they always know the way forward.

She glanced at her herd. Surprisingly, they were all safe and silently standing at attention. Like her, they seemed to be sizing up the mysterious stranger.

The man continued, his voice mellow and mesmerizing. "I come bearing two gifts. May I approach?"

Laila hesitated then nodded. She locked eyes with Mincaye. The fire roared, and she glimpsed the flames dancing in his eyes. He hid his parcel away again and stepped across the river rock, never once taking his eyes from hers.

Once he had arrived at her camp, she motioned for him to sit across from her on the verdant green of the woodland floor. He rolled out a wool rug festooned with trees and flowers flanking a river. Mincaye stretched out on it and accepted the tea she offered. After several moments of sipping in silence and curiously observing one another, he extracted a vibrant textile cloth from his cloak and untied a burlap bundle to reveal a cacao shell full of lipstick-pink squares. He held it out to her, and said, "Ruby delight."

Popping a pink chocolate chunk in her mouth, Laila groaned. "Mmmm...a delicious berry treasure."

"Treasure indeed." He winked and held up another chocolate chunk. "Would you care for another...berry?"

Her face lit up with pleasure. "Yes!" She closed her eyes and held out her hand. Suddenly, her eyes flew open when she felt his hand on top of hers. His fist was coiled around something, but she couldn't tell if it was the chocolate or something else.

"I thought you were giving me another ruby morsel."

He smiled. "Ruby, yes. Morsel? Well, I'll let you decide."

Mincaye slowly placed his other hand over his heart at the same time he opened his fist. Something cold and round now sat in the middle of her palm. Laila held it aloft to catch the firelight and realized she was staring at a stunning star ruby the size of a robin's egg. Her mouth agape, she turned to face him.

"Laila, you are the jewel I have searched for and finally found. My dreams of you in a faraway land came true. I just had to follow a Christmas star to Kashmir."

The Day of the Play

by

Kitt Patten

Ronnie and Maria chattered behind me, and I shushed them. I opened the door to my parent's office at the back of the aircraft hangar. There was a large wooden desk, a four-drawer metal filing cabinet, and an old couch that my dad and I were known to sneak a nap on. My dad was up flying with a student and Mom had gone off to get groceries, but I couldn't throw off the feeling that we needed to be quiet, and hurry. I turned on the gooseneck desk lamp and bent the head up so more of its light fell on the couch. I motioned them into the office and shut the door behind them.

"Here." I'd brought my beach towel along and I handed it to Maria. "You're the nurse."

"Do I have lines to say?" Maria asked.

Yes, if you make them up as we go along."

I turned to Ronnie. "That leaves you as the patient." Because really, he was the point of this little play we were putting on. I was pretty sure I knew what Maria looked like under those pink shorts of hers, because I'd looked at myself down there, with mom's little hand mirror she kept in the second drawer.

Yesterday, Frank Lessing had whispered to me, by the water fountain at the pool, that boys had a thing hanging down, down there. And even worse, he said his older brother had said that boys fit into girls somehow. I thought maybe Frank was lying, but if he wasn't, I just had to see this thing.

"So, Ronnie, in this play, you've fallen out of a tree, and we are here to check that you are okay. I'm playing Doctor Amelia and Maria here, is my trusty nurse. Your leg is

"I wished our play had made it to the final act."

hurting you something awful, so we need to check if you've broken any bones. We'll turn around while you take off your pants. We'll use the couch for the examination. Put the towel over your...middle...," I motioned for Maria to give him my towel, "and let us know when you're ready."

Ronnie started to sputter about having to be the patient, and I reminded him that it was my idea, and besides, it was two against one, so he'd better get out of those jeans. I turned around and so did Maria and we shut our eyes tight. I could hear the rustling of his pants coming off.

"Don't forget your underwear," I said, in my best stern doctor voice. "You could be badly hurt. We have to check everything."

"Okay. I'm ready," he said, in his little-boy whine.

Maria and I turned around. She was standing close to me, and I could feel her arm shaking a bit where it touched mine. I could see his white briefs on top of his wadded-up jeans, next to his leather sandals so the plan was working. I took charge and stepped to the couch.

"Does it hurt here?" I whispered loudly, squeezing around one ankle. "Or here?" He twitched and giggled each time I touched his tanned skin. I tried to say doctorly things as I went along. "Seems to be no breaks in this leg bone...kneecap is okay...no bones sticking out of his thigh..."

I'd examined everything up to the towel. My heart was pounding in my ears, and I pulled Maria up next to me. I lifted the towel and threw it up over his face.

"Hey!" he said, but he stayed still.

We stood there looking at the small worm of a thing lying between his legs, or at least I did. I think Maria was still trying to figure out what she was supposed to be doing as the nurse. I took a deep breath then and reached to touch the one thing I most wanted to examine.

From behind me, I heard my mother say "Amelia!" as she turned on the overhead light. "What are you doing?"

We froze for a half a second of stupid surprise, then we were scrambling. Ronnie pushed the towel off his head and down over his privates. Maria started flinging her arms around and moving in little circles, like she'd run away if she only knew which direction to go, then she stopped and burst into tears. I turned and put myself between Mom and the worst of Ronnie, so maybe, just maybe, she wouldn't see.

"Amelia. Maria. Come with me. Ronnie. Get dressed and go home." Mom belted out the orders like a drill sergeant with new recruits. She grabbed my arm hard, but I didn't dare to complain, and marched us girls to the large open hangar door and out onto the tarmac.

She stopped and we stopped, like good little soldiers. She searched the sky - I guessed for my father's plane. I looked, too, and didn't see it or hear it. Mom exhaled in a huff.

"Go home, Maria."

Maria skittered away, toward the opening in the chain link fence that surrounded the airfield, boo-hooing as she went.

Mom pulled me toward the house. Once inside, she flung me toward the couch. I sat down hard and stared at my feet.

"Stay here until your father lands. I guarantee, you don't want me to deal with you."

I heard her stomp away from me. I lifted my eyes and watched her grab her purse off the kitchen table. She went out the open front door, slamming it hard as she left. I heard her car start up and leave.

I fell over onto my side on the couch, drawing my knees tight into my chest. The house was silent, except for my muttering, "stupid, stupid, stupid." My hand still wanted to feel what I hadn't gotten to touch, and even as part of me regretted my stupid scheme, I wished our play had made it to the final act.

I stayed on the couch, not moving, waiting on my father. When he saw me there, he'd come and sit next to me, probably stroke my hair, and ask me what was wrong. He wouldn't know what had happened. He wouldn't know that I'd done it this time, that I'd finally made my mother stop loving me.

The Adventures of Begonia Honey DeeVine

by

Sally McGee

Sitting in the classroom her mind wandered. Whatever the teacher was talking about was of no interest to Begonia. She was thinking about her cousin, Madeline, and the return of LeRoy, Jr. from a South Texas prison. Mama Beckworth had sent him out for a loaf of bread and that was the last anyone had seen of him for five years. LeRoy was supposed to be Madeline's Daddy or so her Mama, June Bell, said. Le Roy had another opinion. He wanted his bedroom back but Madeline and June Bell were firmly ensconced. Now tension was high and everyone on guard.

Mama Beckworth had little respect for her son.

"He was always a ne'er do well but one with charm. No more! Prison made the bad worse and the good disappear," she flatly stated. Begonia worried about Madeline. She knew what it was like to have a father abruptly appear. The war ended and Capt. Andy had entered her life a complete stranger and moved the family to the Upcountry. She still longed for her old life and missed Granddaddy's big backyard, Willie, Twigger and Azalee.

But for Madeline things were more complicated. LeRoy, Jr. was supposed to be her Dad but he sure did not act like any Dad Begonia knew. Mama Beckworth laid down the law. LeRoy had to contribute. No one was waiting on him hand and foot. LeRoy studied the problem and was now investigating get rich quick schemes while also considering being a Bible salesman. To Sadie Mae, who worked for the Beckworth family, that seemed a ridiculous proposition and she did not hesitate to make her disdain known.

"Nobodies gon buy anything from you," she declared.

LeRoy frowned. He did not like being told what to do by Sadie Mae or anyone else.

Beckworth expected him to step up, get a job, be a man but she and everyone else knew that might not be possible.

Begonia twiddled her thumbs and stared out the classroom window. If only she could sprout wings and fly. Sadly her attempts had ended in abysmal failure. Thankfully the bell rang. As always, she was first out the door. Walking home she could not help noticing the goody two shoes, Candace. Her neighbor was playing tea party and had set up a small table and chairs beneath the Magnolia tree. Carefully she lifted a small cup to her doll's face encouraging "Dottie" to drink. Then offered her a lemon cookie, the top crusty with sugar. Begonia slowed her step. Those lemon cookies sure looked good. What should she do? It would be easy to take a cookie or three and give Candace the good slapping she so deserved. But that would entail tears and loud sobbing and might even mean a telephone call to Capt. Andy. He had a temper and was quick to remove his belt. Munching on the lemon cookie she'd swiped, she walked home.

Dragging her feet, she approached the house. Pushing open the door, silence greeted her. Throwing her book bag onto a chair, she entered the kitchen to make a peanut butter snack. The ringing of the phone broke her reverie. Madeline's voice bubbled with excitement . . .

"You must come to the farm for a visit this week end. Do you think Capt. Andy will bring you? Ten baby pigs were born last night and we can ride Moses the mule. Please say yes."

It seemed to take forever but finally the week end arrived. Capt. Andy drove the Studebaker up a long drive with pasture gone to weed on both sides. The farm house came into view. It was big with a wrap-a-round porch that badly needed a fresh coat of paint. The chimney leaned hard to the left. The family stood on the porch watching as the car approached. Immediately

Begonia spotted Madeline. The girls wasted no time with the adults. Madeline was excited to show off the baby pigs. Leaning over the stall rail, they watched as all ten piglets nestled close struggling to find a teat and feed. They were still too young to hold, according to Mama Beckworth.

Madeline volunteered,

"We have a mule named Moses. I 'spose we could ride him. He is real tall. When he rubs his back on the apple tree, we could jump on."

Without a moment's hesitation, the girls were off making a bee-line for the apple tree. Climbing the tree was not a problem. It was the leap and the landing. This was the third attempt. Each time they came close but as if Moses knew something untoward was going to happen, he took a side step and they landed in the dirt. Now sitting in the tree glaring hard at each other, Madeline was ready to ditch the plan and go on to something new. Begonia dug in her heels. She dreamed of riding a pony and sailing high over Grandmother's forsythia bush in Granddaddy's backyard. Now riding Moses, the mule was as close to realizing her dream as she'd ever come and she was not giving up. She felt inclined to draw back her fist and give Madeline a good punch in the nose but angry energy was rising from her cousin. Begonia hesitated.

"Just one more time. I know we can make it work. Hold tight to my waist." she instructed. "That's what you said last time."

Madeline was getting annoyed at this know it all. The sound of movement caused both girls to look down. Helplessly they watched as Moses ambled off. Dropping to his knees he rolled in the dirt massaging his hips in the warm earth. Standing he shuttered hard. Dirt and dust rose in the air. Slowly he walked to the creek. Lowering his head, he took a long, cool drink.

Jumping from the tree, Madeline yelled,

"Race you to the barn," and she was off with a clear head start.

On the ride home Begonia thought about the day. She was excited to have a cousin, another girl who liked the same things. Not a prissy girl afraid of getting dirty. A run and jump kind of girl. Capt. Andy gunned the engine and the Studebaker responded. Speeding home she reflected, it had been a good day. The farm reminded her of her life before Capt. Andy in Granddaddy's backyard. There she lived with chickens, a cow, a bull named John Henry. In a world where the weather turning cool meant hog killing time. She missed all that. City living could not compare.

Now if only Capt. Andy agreed, she would be a regular visitor to the Beckworth family farm.

"This time I'll come back with the goods and the Royal Archaeological Society will finally admit me as a member."

Dig Under Where?
(With Apologies to Indiana Jones)

by

James Scott

Globe-trotting rebel archaeologist Random Diggs tugged his battered fedora lower on his sweaty brow and tried to concentrate on the interlocking stones of the ancient wall before him. Finally, he thought, after fruitless goose chases on five continents, he was surely only feet from his goal--the discovery of the fabulous, oft-rumored Froom treasure, the last remnant of a long-vanished mysterious culture. Licking his lips, he turned for an instant to his trusted aide, Vietnamese whiz-kid geologist Ho Li Cao.

"Cao," he said, voice raspy in the semi-dark of the long underground tunnel, "this is the payoff. This is where we see if this code I got in Rangoon is the real thing."

Ho Li Cao grinned. "Hope so, boss. You had to kill three people for it."

"No great loss. They needed killing."

"I know you good, boss," Ho Li Cao replied. "You're still sweating it out wondering if the Major beat you to the prize."

"Damn your eyes, Cao, don't remind me. That blasted woman has been one step ahead of me for years. But not this time. Who else could possibly know to dig here, underneath the Temple of Karnak?"

But his mind admitted a shadow of doubt. Major Ophelia Bazooms, beautiful daughter of the president of the Royal Archaeological Society, was his nemesis, dogging his footsteps all over the globe, using her alluring beauty to buy favors and gain influence, and continually getting away with the prize treasure.

"From Bangkok to Bombay," Diggs continued sourly, "from Hogarth to Helsinki, she and that stacked assistant of hers--Moana Lott--have gotten away with the best stuff."

"It's Monica Lot, boss," Li Cao said.

Diggs smiled slyly. "Moana is more appropriate, trust me."

Li Cao gave Diggs a curious look. "You never mentioned Helsinki."

"Never mind. Best left unsaid." He turned his gaze back to the rock wall. "But no way Bazooms could know about this," he said defiantly. "This time I'll come back with the goods and the Royal Archaeological Society will finally admit me as a member. The Froom treasure is mine."

He consulted the worn scrap of parchment in his hand for a few seconds in the dim torchlight, then turned it over and studied it again. Then he reached out and delicately rearranged five pieces of stone in the wall. Two seconds after the last stone was in place, there was a click, a puff of dust, and the wall slid aside.

There was a dark chamber on the other side. Diggs held his torch high and climbed carefully through the opening. The flickering light revealed a collection of dusty artifacts. Diggs looked them over, rubbing his chin. He had been right! They bore the unmistakable style of the lost civilization of the Froom. Feverishly he looked around for the greatest prize, what would be the capstone of his career--the legendary Necklace of Aphrodite. It was rumored to be a huge emerald slung on a gold chain, and said to be looped around a gold-plated bust.

He swept the torch around the room. There was the bust! He reached for it--and his heart sank. The necklace was gone! There clearly had been something around the bust's neck, judging from a pattern devoid of dust. The treasure had been looted! Someone had been there, and recently, too. Gone, and with it his hopes for the triumph of his career. Morosely, he sank to his knees, then sat with a thud amid the artifacts. Sure, they might be valuable, but nothing that would give him the triumph he wanted.

"Tough luck, boss," Ho Li Cao said through the opening in the wall. "We can only hope the Major didn't beat us to it."

"No way," Diggs said with resignation, wiping his brow. "Just no way."

A month later the two were back in London at the annual meeting of the Royal Archaeological Society. He had dressed in his best tux, hoping it would help him feel better about coming back, by his standards, empty-handed. Champagne glass in hand, he stood morosely by the table of hors d' oeuvres, surveying the crowd. "No sign of the Major," he said to Ho Li Cao. "That's something, anyway."

"Yeah, boss, but Moana-| mean Monica--came in, and went back out a moment ago."

Diggs looked away across the room, and his expression darkened. Monica Lott had come back--and she wasn't alone. "Moana's back. And she's got Major Bazooms."

"I'll say," Li Cao said brightly. "I figure her for a D-cup, easy."

"That's not what I meant, and you know it," Diggs replied sourly.

Ophelia Bazooms saw him from across the room. She strolled up to him with the grace of a lioness and stopped three feet away, tossing her blond hair. "Random Diggs," she said sweetly. "Heard your little expedition in North Africa came up dry."

"Not that you care," Diggs said acidly.

"Well," she said, smiling, "I just wanted you to know I had better luck." She pulled open her elegant evening jacket.

Diggs' heart sank to his shoes, his worst fears realized. He knew this time he could never forgive her. For about her slender neck was looped a gold necklace. At its end hung a huge emerald pendant, sparkling in the light. He had no doubt--it was the Necklace of Aphrodite. The style, the craftsmanship--they could mean only one thing. She was indeed wearing loot of the Froom.

"The loud chaos echoes Jasmine's mood, falling and lifting, and screeching out joy and despair."

Leaving Home

by

Jill Elliott

"Soon, you must leave." The mother keeps her eyes on the potatoes she's peeling to avoid looking directly at her daughter. "I don't like the way his eyes follow you around the room or the way he pulls you onto his lap of an evening."

"I'll go my room straight after dinner so I don't have to sit on his lap." It's obvious to Jasmine who he is; the latest of the handful of men she'd been told to call uncle since her father died. "Or I'll hide in the woods until he's asleep." Jasmine fears getting lost in the woods after dark, more than fears leaving the only home she's ever known.

"Has he touched you underneath your clothes?" The mother half-fills a saucepan of potatoes with water, adds a pinch of salt, and sets the pot on the stove.

There was no right answer. If she tells the truth the mother would likely slap her and tell her she is to blame for encouraging him.

"No," Jasmine lies. She bends her head over the book she's reading.

The mother turns away from the stove to focus on her daughter's red cheeks. She sighs heavily. "You're not telling me the truth," she says. "Go upstairs and pack some clothes in the rucksack. Save room for your favorite things, but remember, you'll be the one carrying the bag tomorrow morning."

How can the mother be so cold? Have bits of her heart chipped away after her husband died, and do more pieces shed as each man leaves? The mother keeps no space in her heart for her daughter.

A list of things to carry into the woods:

  1. A journal and five colored pens

  2. Water

  3. Brightly colored ribbons

  4. Clothes

  5. A walking stick with a hooked end for berry picking

  6. A glass jar with a lid – for honey should the bees wish to share

  7. A gathering basket

Jasmine's fears were coming true. She'd be alone tomorrow with no family to count on. Not merely abandoned but pushed out of the nest so young. Surely there was a law that said parents weren't allowed to shove their children out until they were fully grown. She hears the uncle stomping around the cottage. He's a woodcutter who works from dawn to dusk. When he's home, she and her mother tiptoe around him, fearing his sudden rage. He's easily roused to anger.

She hears the door slam soon after the sky lightens to day and knows the man has left. Downstairs the mother snores on the couch, an empty vodka bottle on the floor. She wakes with a loud snort and pulls herself into a slumped sitting position. Jasmine fetches a couple of aspirin and a glass of cold water and hands them to the mother.

"Is he here?"

Jasmine peers out the window at the empty driveway. "He's gone."

"Then you'd better go too. Is your bag packed?"

Jasmine nods and steps into the kitchen to pour a bowl of cereal with milk. She doesn't know when she'll eat again. The mother splashes orange juice into a large tumbler and sets it in front of her daughter.

"Listen carefully. Walk with your back to the sun, and when the sun is high above, find shelter and rest a while. I've heard tell of a kind woman who shelters people who need a safe place to stay. Follow the sun until it sets. You might have to spend a night in the woods, but if you keep heading west the next day, you'll likely find her, or she'll find you."

Jasmine wants to argue with the mother, but knows from past experience that it would be a waste of time and probably lead to shouting. The mother hands her two apples and a chunk of bread. Both of them have tears in their eyes when Jasmine heads out of the door. She doesn't look back.

A list of questions Jasmine never asked her mother:

1. Why don't you send this uncle away instead of me?
2. Where does his anger come from?
3. Will I ever see you again?
4. If I were a boy, could I have stayed?
5. Are you going to replace me with another child?
6. Why do your eyes leak tears?
7. Did you ever love me?

She walks fast letting anger set her pace. Jasmine rips a piece of bread from the loaf and chews it. She drops breadcrumbs here and there in case the unwritten rules of her life change and she can return to the place called home. She ties red and blue ribbons to branches and hears the chirp of a robin, the screech of a jay. Jasmine walks until the sun is directly overhead and finds a bed of moss. Using her rucksack as a pillow she drifts into a light sleep.

She wakes with a start when something drops onto her forehead. "Ouch," she says to no one at all. Then she remembers; the mother told her to leave, she's in the woods and she's supposed to head west until she finds a wise woman. Instead, she's eye to eye with a squirrel. The rodent with the bushy tale is doing that cute thing, where it sits on its hind legs, nibbling at a nut trapped between its front paws. Impossible not to smile.

Moving as slowly as possible, Jasmine pulls an apple from her pocket. The squirrel watches as she takes one bite, and then another. Her parched throat appreciates the juiciness of the fruit. Jasmine places the core on her open hand and leans towards the squirrel. It drops the nut it's been nibbling, grabs the apple core and retreats a few steps. Out of Jasmine's reach it devours the fruit.

The sun is much lower than the girl expected. Shadows lengthen as she follows a path through the brush. She feels lighter with each step she takes away from the mother, freer, ready to start a life of her own. Then she reminds herself she's nine and she's only got one apple and a chunk of bread left to eat. The abundant blackberry brambles she sees are heavy with green berries and will take all summer to ripen.

Crows caw in tall Douglas firs. Jasmine caws back at them, and soon a cacophony of harsh cries fills the woods. She smiles and screeches again and then laughs loudly. The crows screech even louder. A murder of crows, she thinks, maybe they'll find the latest uncle and end his life. Then she could return to the mother. But the crows stay with her, flying in short bursts away from the sun. They circle in tall trees, landing briefly, then flying again. The loud chaos echoes Jasmine's mood, falling and lifting, and screeching out joy and despair.

A fox, walks slowly ahead as if daring her to follow. She's mesmerized by its tail, the point on the end like a beacon. Jasmine follows it along a path. Sometimes the fox stops and turns its head as if to make sure she's still there. Jasmine's new life began today with a sense of adventure she's never felt before. Her basket remains empty. You cannot fill a basket with scents of newly opened violets, the sparkle of leaves in sudden sunshine, or the wind rustling through trees.

The fox is following the request of the woman who lives in the last cottages at the edge of the forest. They communicate without words. She wants this girls to visit a fallen oak tree, one of the many with entangled roots. Yet this tree's roots leads to other worlds. A magical tree with powers that only the dead can hold.

As the sun sinks the crows roost on tall trees and their cries subside. Jasmine knows they watch her and feels protected. She stumbles over a tree root and sits down hard. From her perch on the ground she notices a hollow in the roots of a massive fallen oak. Ferns grow on the decaying bark and mushrooms emerge through thick undergrowth. She snuggles deep under the tangle of tree roots and soon sleeps.

A wolf howls in the distance. A bald eagle flies high. A mouse crunches dry leaves.

Tim

by

Constance Smith

Dear Tim,

I just found out, way late. I ran across the poem on a fluke. It brought up memories. And tears. I saw that you were married. By the looks of your photos, you were happy. I'm glad.

You and my mother had a great time together working in her garden. You never kissed me, not even my cheek, but you kissed hers. And you kissed our dog when you carried him around, and talked to him like he was a baby. My father didn't have much to say to you. He never talked to babies or dogs, or guys who were interested in cucumbers. But you and he did have that one good conversation, when you told him your family owned a plumbing business. He was cool with anything to do with business, especially owning.

At lunch you sat with our group, Cathy, Lori, Beth, and me. All the girls liked you. And you liked them. But I was the one you went with. You never made my heart race like Alan did, but you and I were more than friends for a whole summer. At least that's how I felt about it then, and I thought you did too. We hung out at the lake. You taught me how to slalom and jump the wake. It was fun walking across the bridge to Village Pizza. You gave me that gold name bracelet. Not the same as a ring, but still special.

We used to lie on the grass and talk about names, how they conjured up colors in our minds. Timothy was green, celadon to you, more like lime to me, but green nonetheless. Cathy and Lori were both white. Beth was orange. We went down the alphabet and agreed on just about all of them. It was eerie. Though I remember that Sindy was yellow to you but gray to me.

It wasn't a formal thing, so we never broke up. We just sort of drifted apart. Then Alan asked me out. You weren't one bit jealous. You even came over a couple of times and hung out with us on the patio. We ate popsicles and talked about the future. Alan wanted to go to law school someday. You wanted to have a farm and plant an orchard.

That was so long ago. Late 60s. Back when reading minds and reading between the lines were survival skills. It seemed there was a stigma attached to just about everything. Mental breakdown, physical disability, failing in school— stigmas all around. Unmarried at 30, stigma. Single and pregnant, big fat stigma.

And it wasn't something you could shake off. Once it was on you, it stuck, and you would have to go into a coma or move to Timbuktu to escape it. And it was contagious. Part of it jumped onto your parents, your siblings, anyone who associated with you. Stigmas about race, religion, occupations, and who knows what all. So many stigmas that if you didn't have one, you could get one almost overnight, and you wouldn't even have to work at it.

Analyzing them was complicated. Sometimes you had no idea where they came from. They could shape-shift from halfway permissible to intolerable, depending on who wore them and who assigned them. Certain ones were more damning than others, depending on who you were talking to.

Just look at my family. They shunned Aunt Kay because she had Holly when she wasn't married. There was a stigma on Holly because she was her mother's daughter. You might remember my cousin, Hank. He was two years behind us in school. He got his stigma the night he tried to hang himself. But there was worse. Uncle Martin was intimate with a woman of another race, not to mention all those loose women up at the lake house—so no way was he getting by without a stigma. Uncle Roy cheated on Aunt Lucille. But when he started staying up at the lake house with Uncle Martin, the stigma he already had, at least doubled. Hank was still single in his forties and had mostly lived down his suicide stigma. Then he moved in with his gentleman friend. Not only did that smack him with a new stigma, but it brought his old one back to life, bigger than ever.

A lot of pretending went on. Lies. Being found out. Hiding. It drains me to think about how things used to be. People are more accepting these days. Except for politics. It's brutal. Consider yourself lucky not to have to deal with it.

I flew out for the ten-year reunion, but I didn't get to see you. Cathy couldn't make it either. Beth was there. Lori acted really strange. Beth told me you were still single, working in the office at the plumbing business, and that you weren't able to be there because you had tickets to see Reba McEntire in Charlotte. I don't blame you. I would have gone to the concert too. That was the first and last reunion I attended. School reunions are about comparisons, pride, and envy—all exhausting propositions.

I searched for you right away when I signed on to Facebook. I guess it was around 2014. Also, without thinking, I picked the Like button on a controversial post, caught a lot of flak for it, then regretted ever getting into it. I couldn't figure out how to delete my account, so I simply stopped using it and moved the icon off my taskbar. I had intended to friend you but never did.

Just yesterday I decided to bring up Facebook, so I could follow a couple of groups I'm in. The Meetup app is a mess. I found you again. I had forgotten that your middle name was Michael. Green, more like shamrock to me. I read what your husband posted on your page, after the cancer stole you. He was openly heart broken. Jeremy, deep red to me. His poem was a lovely tribute. The photo of you under the blooming cherry tree warmed my heart. You volunteered at the Boys' and Girls' Club, and the animal shelter. I'm not surprised.

I'm writing to you, but it's only for me. I know you can't see this, and you aren't looking down on me as I write it, because I don't believe in heaven or the supernatural—it's okay if you did—like ghosts or communing with the dead. Or Jesus, burnt sienna to me.

I hope you weren't in pain. Love,

Sindy

NONFICTION

"I think I was supposed to feel special, singled-out from the crowd of five kids gathered around those bags. Instead, I felt dread."

Hostess Pie

by

Georgianna Marie

My father somehow got it into his mind that I loved Hostess pies. The chocolate ones. Once a month, the Saturday after payday, Dad and Mom would visit the day-old bakery shop, looking for bargains, searching for ways to afford to feed the seven of us for the next 28 days.

After being gone for what seemed like hours, there they'd be, pulling onto the driveway in the car du jour. One month it would be a brand-new, lemon-yellow Mercury Monterrey; the next, a forest green Plymouth hardtop; the next, a station wagon borrowed from the neighbors, or a nondescript used car bought on the fly, in cash, from the corner lot up the street. If they were traveling in style, in one of the newer cars, there would be more bags to dig through, more hopes of tasty treasures. If the Mercury or the Plymouth had gone missing, another victim of repossession, there'd be fewer bags. Either way, there would be a single chocolate pie. For me.

My father would burrow down through a bag of stale Wonder Bread and roughed-up hot dog buns, pulling out that custard-filled, doughy half-moon with a flourish, its waxy wrapping making ominous crinkling noises between his long, skinny fingers.

"Voila," his smile seemed to announce, "I got this just for you!"

I think I was supposed to feel special, singled-out from the crowd of five kids gathered around those bags. Instead, I felt dread.

Only four years old, I'd already learned that it was best to like what Dad offered, that nothing good could come of telling the truth. Instead, I'd say thank you and beg to eat that gooey crescent right away, because I knew that's what he expected, what he wanted. Under his watchful eye, I'd gag down its pudding-like innards and pasty-sweet crust, all the while wishing for the pillowed, spongy lightness of a cream-filled Twinkie – even an outdated, slighted dented, rejected Twinkie. That, I would like. That, I could get behind.

If he knew I hated those things, he didn't care. He'd decided I liked them, so I did. He maybe even reveled in my reticence, enjoyed this game of pretend we played every few weeks. He was amused; he was entertained; he was in control.

This was a pattern of his, maybe even what might be considered his parenting style. It delighted in presenting things his children didn't want or need, then silently declaring the offering somehow heroic. Like, "Look at me. I bought my little girl a chocolate pie, even though money is running short." Our job, as his children, was to be grateful. So, we pretended to be.

At worst, he'd not just bestow things (like pies) on a kid, but demand things of a kid, all in the spirit of fun and in service to his amusement. These small cruelties took place in the light of day, within earshot of our mother and each other. We'd watch; we'd listen; we'd learn; we'd divine what was expected of us.

I have very few memories of time spent with my father, but one stands out. I call it the "hand crunch." Every so often, from his perch on the couch, he'd beckon me over, grinning his chocolate-pie smile, telling me he had something fun he wanted to show me. He'd be there with one of his favorite snacks, like the Bugles he was always eating. One of my three older sisters would be sidled up next to him on the couch, dutifully filling those Bugles with peanut butter – the crunchy kind, which he preferred. The sister would hand over Bugles, one after the other, as he took them in, washing them down with noisy gulps from the can of Schlitz at his side.

I didn't know then, and wouldn't find out for years, what was really happening on that couch but, when my father beckoned, I'd approach shyly, the way a kid would with a stranger or visitor to the house. In my internal movie of this scene, he feels like someone I'm only vaguely familiar with, and not too comfortable being around.

In that reel, he appears and disappears from scene-to-scene without explanation, sometimes present and often not.

This, I suppose, is how my four-year-old mind tried to make sense of his moods. In reality, during my first four or five years, he was usually there in body, but often absent in mood and spirit. So, when Dad was smiling and offering you a pie or a Bugle-filling post, or signaling you over to the couch, a girl would take it; a girl would go. This is as good as it got.

So. He'd lure me over, then clasp my tiny hand between the span of his lanky fingers. Holding my palm flat in his, he'd squeeze the pinkie knuckle against the ring-finger knuckle, then the ring-finger knuckle against the middle finger knuckle, and so on, in an accordion-like crushing motion.

It hurt.

I'd yank my hand away, shaking and rubbing it, while he chuckled in the background. "I told you it would be fun," he'd say.

Like the pie scenario, I'd smile. I'd pretend to like his game. I'd play it again when, a few weeks later, we'd repeat the dance anew, me falling for his promise of "fun" over and again.

He spent a lot of time on that couch, reading the newspaper, watching TV, and snacking. When it wasn't Bugles, it was the sardines, another weapon in his parenting arsenal. He loved the oily, smelly, slimy little creatures laid out on Saltine crackers. He loved them even more if he could manipulate one of the kids into preparing each cracker for him. Better yet if he could convince a girl that she wanted to do this for him, if he could demand it yet lead her to believe it was an honor, that she was special.

I barely remember any of this, but my siblings report that we all (Mom included) thought this was a disgusting snack and couldn't bear the smell permeating the house. Luckily for me, I was too young to undertake sardine cracker duty. My sisters though, took it on, with the same measure of dread I experienced with each chocolate pie.

His demands that we participate in ways none of us wanted – there, out in the open – were just his front line of attack. He used these to teach us how to go along, how to pretend to enjoy what he was offering, and how to keep quiet and never admit the truth. Over time, he would leverage these tactics to single each of us out, to create the impression that each of us, in turn, was somehow special, chosen over the others. Taking us from out-in-the-open to behind-closed-doors, where he could demand anything he wanted. In return, he expected us to like it, or at least pretend we did. He expected us to stay silent, never revealing the truth.

Just like those times he brought me a chocolate Hostess pie.

"I was curious, open to an unlikely experience, a story to tell, a glimpse of a possible future."

The Psychic

by

Sue McGrath

Nothing in my belief system gives credence to the concept of a set path in life, a life preordained. So why would I go to a psychic? No one can know the future, right?

"It's an otherworldly experience," Maggie and Reggie gushed. "It'll blow your mind."

The psychic, Michael Thompson, had a talent, a gift. They all agreed. What is it exactly? No one could say. Intuition? Theatrics? Empathy? A great reader of demographics? Or is he truly psychic? Able to see your future?

Sheila told me her experience:

Michael began by saying he saw her child, a girl.

"I have a child. A boy."

He shook his head, looking at her through his peripheral vision. "Hmm. I strongly sense the presence of a girl."

Sheila didn't know it, but she was pregnant with a girl.

And so I went. Why not? I was curious, open to an unlikely experience, a story to tell, a glimpse of a possible future.

Michael did readings in his parlor, a cozy room up a narrow stairway, in a tattered Victorian in NW Portland. He sat at a small round table draped with a purple floor length cloth, and adorned with a crystal ball and tarot cards. He didn't appear to use either prop, though he may have occasionally turned over a card and glanced down at it. He wore a colorful cape draped over his shoulders. He looked toward me but not at me, mid-distance, light blue eyes unfocused, head slightly tipped to the left, like a blind man.

Toward the end of my reading he said, "You see yourself as living to a very old age."

I did.

He shook his head, sadly. "Do you want me to tell you at what age you will die?"

I should have said no. Why didn't I say no?

For years I didn't think about it. The number was still far away. At times when I was in a harrowing situation I'd allowed myself to believe in the number: "I will get through this. It is not my year to die."

Now, that number looms large, gathering mass and density. I search my mind for all the things Michael Thompson got wrong but I remember the things he got right.

Though I met with him in Portland, he knew right away I lived in the country, on 10 acres he said. No, it was 5 acres. But still.

He asked me about my sisters, especially the youngest one. "You're very close," he said.

I told him I was 11 years older. She was 7 when I set off for college and life beyond. I loved her, but we were not close.

"You will get very close. I see her living under your roof for an extended period of time." He couldn't tell me why or when exactly, but he saw it clearly.

That seemed unlikely, but when my sister was 18 and pregnant she lived with us. She was trying to keep her pregnancy secret from family and friends back in the Midwest. She planned to give the baby up for adoption. I was her LaMaze coach, myself 5 months pregnant. The night before her water broke, she decided she could not give up the baby. The bonds of our mutual pregnancies and childbirth extended to child rearing. We shared the woes, the wonders, and the hilarious stories.

My husband had a reading with Michael Thompson after our first child was born. Michael predicted that we would have two children, and the second would be a boy just like the first. When Bob told Michael our firstborn was a girl, he shook his head perplexed and said, "Well, they will both be good children." Our first born now identifies their gender as non-binary.

I used to have a crumpled sheet of lined yellow paper on which I wrote everything I remembered that Michael said to me and to Bob. In our many moves that paper is long gone. How I wish I had it. How I wish I could review and laugh over the many things the psychic got oh so wrong. He must have gotten things wrong, right?

I worry about the power of suggestion. Placebo and nocebo effects are real. The extent of the power of the mind to hurt and to heal the body are unknown. And so I play a game with myself; I remind myself I don't believe anyone can truly see the future, though one might make exceptionally good guesses based on statistics, demographics, likelihoods, hunches. I don't believe the future is fixed. I offer myself alternative suggestions of a long life. But I feel Michael Thompson's prediction like a stone in the gray matter of my brain.

Don't ask me the number. I will not tell you. To repeat it is to give it power. Let's just say, I am planning a huge celebration if I make it to my next birthday.

ROCKAWAY WRITERS RENDEZVOUS 2024 ANTHOLOGY

Single Girl

by

Eve Whitall

"May-day! May-day! This is N319CS. I'm headed for Pendleton, but off-course and soon out of gas." The pilot's voice choked on his last word.

Charlie and I were still getting to know each other. It was our sixth flight together in his home-built Glasair two-seater. Most were adventures to places I'd never been, areas that encouraged fly-ins: Stehekin, where no roads can take you; Red's Horse Ranch, where I rode "Surprise," Silverwood Theme Park and a little train ride where bandits "robbed" us. And the Odessa Octoberfest, where we grabbed bratwurst and hitchhiked a ride back to the airport at the top of the hill. We were playing grown-up kids.

He was a slender, red-headed cowboy, that Charlie, with grey sideburns and a ready smile that peeked out below a porcupine mustache. Flights with him took me into another world, away from the stresses of a high-profile job.

But one prior flight had not turned out well. That day, Charlie did barrel rolls over the Columbia River immediately after we had lunched at the Kittitas Restaurant. I saw in him a desire to scare me. "Take me back to the airport," I said. "I feel sick." After that, I avoided seeing him for several months.

Time passed; it was early summer, and I accepted his invitation to fly over to Boise to visit my family for the weekend.

The flight over had been enjoyable except for our arrival when Charlie got scolded for making an error in his permission to land. Still, we'd reached the area for small planes, next to gas pumps, without being fined.

We began our return flight under crystalline skies Sunday morning, waving and smiling our goodbyes. "I'll call you when I get home in about two hours," I said to my kids as I climbed in, stretched my legs straight out front on the carpeted floor, and wiggled my headphones to fit.

Charlie zigzagged down the runway, peering around the nose of the tail dragger until we were airborne and the plane leveled off.

"Watch the freeway below and tell me if we get off track," Charlie said.

I tapped the boom mic. "Don't you use instruments?" I asked.

"Naw. Don't need 'um."

I bit my finger, watching the miniature cars below, appearing not to move. Then, I lost sight of the silver winding ribbon.

"Charlie, I can't see any road."

"Yeah, I know. We're being blown off course."

"Do you see anything familiar below?" he asked?

"No, there's nothing but forest. And we should be over the desert and the Snake River. But I don't see it."

How did he hope to find the path home? Charlie would know, wouldn't he? Maybe using his compass or those other gadgets on the dash? If only I could see a building or a road, it would help.

Now, I overhear, we are running out of gas! Why hadn't he filled up when we were in Boise?

Charlie muttered in a monotone voice, "I didn't file a flight plan." His arched nose glistened with sweat in the bright sunlight.

I strained my neck to look below; small patches of sand interspersed large swaths of dark green.

I tapped the boom mic again. "Can't we land on that barren stretch?"

"No, hitting one shrub of tumbleweed will cause the plane to flip," he moaned, looking straight ahead. "WE'RE GOING TO DIE!" His splintered words hit a crescendo, and a tear rolled down his cheek.

Charlie was in a panic. "How can I help?" Sounds bounced off my lips without engaging my brain. I'd never piloted a plane. What if he had a heart attack?

No reply.

"Charlie, it is not my time to die!" I gritted my teeth with determination. I stared at him. "You are going to get this plane landed and refueled."

Like a cattle prod, my words shocked him out of his stupor.

A radio call came in. "N319CS, this is Seattle Control. We have you on our radar. Maintain an altitude of 2,500 feet, take heading 350 degrees, and proceed to Pendleton Airport. You are forty miles out."

My knees quivered, and my heart fluttered, but I believed what I said; it was not my time to die.

Charlie redirected the plane, and within minutes, we headed north. I imagined the last ounces of gasoline flowing through an hourglass with seconds to go. Thirty minutes passed, and like a miracle, we were still in the sky, and the single-engine continued to hum.

Wheat fields loomed ahead.

Then, I-84 was in sight.

Like a desert oasis, the airstrip appeared.

Tan buildings, the terminal, the outline of the bucking horse, his tail held high in the air, the cowboy, his hat flying off but still in the saddle; words, Let 'Er Buck! Such joy, such a wondrous sight!

Neither of us spoke.

The engine sputtered, but the runway was within reach. One more cough from the front of the plane, and then only the sound of air whistling past the wings. We floated like a bird. Charlie's knuckles turned bluish-white as he strangled the wheel.

The tires hit the ground. We bounced and bounced once more. And then came to rest. Not the best landing, but we made it! I opened the door, slid toward the ground, fell to my knees, and kissed the good earth. "Thank you, God," I whispered. Still trembling out of control, unable to stand, I felt like crying. I needed a moment.

At last, I took a deep breath, stood with shaky legs, touched the plane's cold white surface, and thanked the aircraft too. I turned to face Charlie, his hand on the gas pump connected like an umbilical cord to the plane. He smiled a boyish grin. Without reciprocating, I turned and began walking to my car.

He called after me, "That was your initiation. You're ready to start lessons."

His words slid down my back, crashed to the ground, and disintegrated. I got in my car and headed west, alone.

The End

"The room became more crowded with men yelling and arguing and passing money back and forth. I curiously watched not understanding the commotion or intensity of the unfolding events."

El Gallo

by

Hector M. Rodriguez

Grandfather took my hand firmly as we approached an old barn set back against a line of scraggly mesquite trees and prickly pair cactus. The earth was baked and dusty. Dried cow patties littered the ground, no cattle in sight. An ancient wooden corral with missing twisted logs made a surround that held wild mustangs once, was now empty. A tattered and frayed rope with a familiar lasso loop knotted on the end was coiled on a post. It was evening, and the South Texas sun was drawing its last breath from another blistering day and the moon had gone into hiding behind distant clouds hinting of rain. Two vaqueros in worn leather chaps and large brim straw hats were squatting near an empty wooden watering trough: their muffled voices uttering colorful Spanish curse words. The dust was thick and brown and gentle puffs rose as I watched the measured steps of others walking towards the barn.

There was an uncomfortable exhilaration in the air as we stepped into the dimly lit structure. Several oil lanterns were hung on bent nails protruding from aged wooden beams crisscrossing the vaulted ceiling. The beams cast gliding shadows across the dusty floor. Voices of Mexican's erupted as wads of bills held in calloused hands were eagerly traded. Money was handed back and forth, and back again as the pitch of the voices kept rising. It was more money than I had ever seen in my 8 years of life. Grandfather pushed and moved us forward. I felt anxious and excited in anticipation of what was happening. The crowd smelled of sweat. The smell was of labor and difficult lives in the heat of survival. I could see the men, baked brown from the sun; they were the color of the dry earth.

We reached a row of large wooden boxes on one edge of the room. Grandfather lifted me up, set me on a post, and said "espera aqui", wait here. I watched him closely as he made his way across the room searching. I watched as he pulled something out of his pocket. I saw glint of gold. He started talking with a stranger, but the man brushed off the dialogue and turned away. Grandfather moved on to another and started to argue showing a small the gold locket dangling from a chain. The man grabbed the locket opening it up. As he closed the clasp they shook hands. Grandfather made his way back giving me a tentative smile. The room became more crowded with men yelling and arguing and passing money back and forth. I curiously watched not understanding the commotion or intensity of the unfolding events. Dust in the room rose up in billowing folds. Grandfather sat on a crate next to me. I was able to look over all the commotion in the room. Soon after Grandfather returned another man arrived and started to talk. He was friendly. I understood some of the conversation. One of the roosters was name was El Gallo del Diablo, Rooster of the Devil. He said the rooster was stolen from Salinas. A small village deep in the heart Mexico and was smuggled across the Rio Grande River. The man said the rooster had never been beaten. Grandfather shook his head saying he heard about El Gallo del Diablo, but the reigning champion of this area was quite good. His champion was El Maestro, the Master, and had never been beaten. El Maestro had fought 18 fights and left 18 challengers dead in the sand. Grandfather was sure he would be victorious in this battle.

I sat and listened. The roar of the room became deafening. Men were yelling and swearing and pushing and shoving and sweating. Dollar bills were everywhere, trading dirty hands and then disappearing into pockets. After a short while four men came in with two large crates moving thru the crowd. The crates were non-descript, draped in scraps of burlap, but I could tell they were important by the way the crowd of men parted to make room. It became quiet as the men placed the crates at opposite sides of the large circular arena. One crate was placed next to me. I peered in and saw a magnificent rooster. His tail feathers stood tall and proud with a litany of reds, blues, yellows, and greens.

His comb was deep red, scared from previous battles. It displayed arrogantly. I sensed the rooster had no fear. I watched his eyes darting and bouncing from target to target, looking for his challenger thru the wooden slats. His beak was chipped. His voice screamed a screeching pensiveness anticipating the battle to come. I could see sagging wings and scars and missing feathers on his breast. His spurs tied back like double-edged daggers poised to strike. He was a warrior, ready for battle. "El Maestro" Grandfather whispered.

On the other side of the circle, I could hear El Gallo del Diablo screeching his call of intimidation. I watched; men exploded in frenzied excitement. Dollars were collected, arguments ensued, and hands were clasped in agreement. At an appointed time, a signal was given, and crate doors flung open. The roosters charged to the center of the ring and a thick fog of dust rose as their wings beat winds of fiery intimidation towards the other. El Gallo del Diablo was magnificent. He was totally black including his comb, hackle, cape, back, spurs, and claws. He was missing one eye and the other had a scare across the eyelid, which caused him to cock his head in a sideways position, looking for an opening to strike. His spurs were long, like Roman spear points at the ready. El Gallo del Diablo looked evil and wicked, a rooster the devil would own.

I watched in stunned amazement as the roosters attacked and rose far above the dirt floor, screaming and squawking. They voiced torment and torture, gashing at each other as spurs and beaks dealt targeted blows. Feathers flew in chaos as the ring of men cheered and screamed and flailed arms in madding anger as each rooster traded blow after blow. The roosters rose far into the air, separated, and fell in heaps of feathers and flesh into the dirt. Then they charged each other again and again and again, daggers and spear points pirouetting to inflict malicious wounds.

The crowd roared in twisted excitement. I saw my grandfather caught up in the frenzy of the battle. His once soft voice was now yelling in a tormented and anguished primordial pitch of passion. It was a moment I would never forget; it was a passion that eviscerated the image of a calm, sensitive and tender man. I saw Grandfather in a way that changed me forever. I saw a man of war and torture and hurt and pain. He was relishing battle recalling his youth and fevered emotions of a young desperado fighting in the Mexican Revolution striving to survive.

As the roosters fought, I was mesmerized by the excitement and hunger of the crowd. I quickly became one of the cheering masses as the birds continued to rise far above the ring ensnaring the crowd in the blood lust duet of death. I started to cheer as my grandfather was. I wanted to be one with him. I felt confused. It was an experience and feeling I had never known. As the roosters rose into the dust filled air the Maestro sunk a nasty gash into the shiny breast of Diablo and Diablo buried a spear deep into the leg of El Maestro and then into his neck. As they fell back to the earth, El Maestro could not stand, his leg was gashed and broken and bleeding. He could not regain his fighting stance. El Maestro hobbled frantically and spinning in circles looking for balance. As he gyrated and flailed madly, El Diablo rose majestically and drove his spears into the neck and head of El Maestro burying him in the blood caked dirt floor. Then again, and again and again until there was no movement. It was done. The room fell silent.

Amid a quite murmur, El Diablo was collected and put into his crate to heal and journey to the next battle. El Maestro was collected to be thrown on to a trash heap outside of the barn, to decay and rot in the hot Texas sun. Grandfather grabbed my hand as we walked back to the old pickup truck in silence. Once in the truck, he said the locket was his mother's. It contained the only picture of her had. He began to cry. The locket always brought good fortune, but not tonight. As we drove home the old truck rattled thru the night. I saw heat lighting in the far-off clouds, like burning alcohol flashing across the dark sky. I hoped it would rain and cool the heat of the night.

"What a time to move to KY. I was still trying to recover from heatstroke when it finally dawned on me, I was now on a different planet."

I Never Thought I Would...

by

Lisa Maxwell

I have always been fairly open minded. Growing up, I was eager to try most things, although I did have my list of would not's. There was climbing to the top of a mountain, riding a bull, scuba diving (extremely claustrophobic), jumping out of a plane, and marrying a military man. That last one must sound a little out of context from the rest of the "would not's". It was probably due to all of the time spent in San Diego, driving by the Marine Base and seeing all those poor boys, dressed alike, heads shaved, being told every move to make. Nope, not for me. I'm way too much of a rebel!

My Mother always told me, Never say never! But I'm holding strong to the majority of items on my "won't do" list, but marrying a military man has now been crossed off. I joined the Army as a 2nd class citizen, Wife.

Luckily I get along with almost everyone, and really enjoy meeting new people which is a good thing especially when I was plucked out of the only home environment I had ever known, in California no less, and dropped into the middle of an Ozzie & Harriet set in Fort Knox, Ky. The only thing missing on the Army wives were Harriet's pearls. They were in 1950's style housing, most of them didn't work, and there were hoards of children playing in the front yards, running around in circles in the sprinklers because it was August! What a fine time to move to Ky. I was still trying to recover from heatstroke when it finally dawned on me, I was now on a different planet. Most of the wives had married young and the Army was all they had known. They seemed to be fine with all the rules and regulations. Actually they didn't even seem to question them, and kind of cocked there head to one side with an eyebrow raised as if trying to understand what I was saying when I did. I may have only been in my teens when I passed the Base in San Diego, but 20 years later I was still very much a rebel, just an older, wiser one. And this new frontier felt like the Twilight Zone.

My poor husband was a stay within the lines kind of guy, so being in the military worked well with his personality. He isn't one to question things he is told to do or try to persuade others to see how a different way might work better. I do think if he had thought about this aspect of my personality a bit more he might have had second thoughts about marrying me. And unfortunately for him, it reared it's ugly head the first week we arrived on post.

We were staying in Billeting waiting for housing to be assigned. Our first stop after signing in on Post was the housing department to get on the list for housing. I went in assuming that the realtor in charge would show us the houses that were available. We would tell him which ones we thought might work and he would proceed to take us to see them. Ah contrare! I was informed by the Sergeant sitting behind a very scratched khaki colored metal desk that when one opened up, they would call us and give us an hour or so to go look at it and tell them yes or no. No need to panic, it's not like you have to take the first one you see. They will let you say no and they will call you again when the next one opens, but God forbid that one is worse because if you say no to that one, you go to the bottom of the list, and your whole family is stuck in Billiting for who knows how long.

I'm sorry, but that just didn't compute. I managed to gather my composure and ask the Sergeant sweetly if perhaps I could just take a quick look at one that was empty. God knows they were all the same, street after street of duplexes. I just needed to know what the inside looked like so I could figure out what we needed. It was the perfect opportunity to use our time while homeless to get organized. But nooooooo. He said, "I'm sorry Ma'am. We don't allow that." If being told no didn't irritate me enough, being called Ma'am about put me over the edge. I was 32 not 62! Fine, I'll figure out another way.

So while Mark was at work that next day I decided to wander around the neighborhood that we were fairly certain we would be assigned to. I started chatting with one of the wives I ran into, and asked her if she would mind showing me her lovely home. She didn't mind at all, and I managed to smile as if I thought it actually was lovely.

When Mark got home that night, I was so excited to tell him the great news. I assumed he would be so happy for me that I solved that first problem. I was not expecting the horrified look on his face. It really didn't make sense. I didn't shoot someone between the eyes, then step over their lifeless body so I could see the house. None the less he informed me that I had stepped out of line. I chalked it up to his nature to overreact until that weekend. We were at the "Get to know the newbies lawn party" and his Colonel's wife came over for introductions. We were standing with a group of people, and when she heard my name, she grabbed my hand and said "Oh, I've heard about you. You take measures into your own hands, I like that!" I looked over at Mark like, 'See I'm not a liability!' I have to say it was a bit frightening at how that info got out, and not surprisingly he looked less than amused.

I on the other hand was hopeful. Surely if the Colonel's wife liked my spunk, the rules must not be as ridiculous as they seemed. Unless she was another one of these women who had joined this group as a child bride and was now completely brainwashed with only a vague memory of wanting to buck the system. But now as a Colonel's wife there was no going back. I on the other hand had a life as an adult before this. I had been married, divorced, married, divorced, (No, I'm not stuttering.) and a single Mom. I could do crazy things in my previous life like go to the market and walk down the aisles willy nilly. I didn't need arrows in the Commissary telling me which direction to go. I can't tell you how many times I would forget that important rule and be happily pushing my cart down an aisle only to have some Old Retiree (mostly men) come at me from the other direction, block my cart and yell at me for going the wrong way. You would think I had just ran a stop sign and was about to plow into him and maim his entire family. It would take everything I had to not to stop and ask him why he didn't find this rule ridiculous, but I didn't. I would apologize profusely and back my cart out the way I had come.

We would also get written up if our lawns were too high in the summer and if you let icicles hang from your eaves too long in the winter. Having grown up in California that last rule seemed incredibly silly. Could we not just wait for them to melt? Why make more work when nature would eventually take it's course? Might there be special issue clothes to wear while hacking away at these beautiful ice formations, safety goggles perhaps?

If you were outside at 5:00 p.m. and the Army song, sorry forgot what it's called, came on over the loud speakers, you would have to stop, put your hand over your heart, take your hat off if you were wearing one and stand there till it was over. Good luck corralling all the young'uns and get them to hold still. I found myself not venturing out between 5:00 & 5:15 if I didn't have to because I might start giggling and look very disrespectful and immature.

There were many other crazy rules and over my 10 year stint I learned to chuckle about them instead of grit my teeth. I have to say that the other things that came with this life more than made up for it. I met the most wonderful people, and traveled all over the world. My Army friends are now scattered everywhere, and they are more than friends, they are family. You are enveloped into the community as soon as you arrive, and friendships are made quicker and deeper than in my old world. Those were some of the best days of my life and I feel so blessed to have done something I never thought I would.

"If I was lucky enough to dream, the images would turn to a leader of a revolution, a Care Crusader. Along with a cape, a pair of shears to cut through red tape, she has a sidekick, a little dog named Patience."

It's All About the Canine

by

Darlene Zimbardi

Do you know how mean people are the to the elderly?

I'm not talking about the average person, I'm talking about the professionals, Yes, they're over worked, possibly underpaid but these so called caretakers really need to be mean to old folks to make ends meet?

Let me back up.

My mom.

She's eighty-one, recently widowed, then had two heart attacks and a stroke.

Picture this:

She's in her hospital bed, with her dog, Chili, lying next to her, when little Miss Social Worker comes in to inform her that the facility will be dumping her out in a couple of days. This Kewpie doll come to life, lays out the assisted living options. "We like to call them ALF's, makes them seem friendlier," she continues, "St. Joe's doesn't allow dogs. St. Pete's, I don't know." She, looks down, "is the dog a deal breaker?"

My mom begins to cry, the dog, whine.

Really? This woman feels totally comfortable waltzing in, telling an old lady whose husband just died, who's so sick she can't even go back home to say goodbye to friends -- I'm going to rip your pet away from you too. Jeez us Chr iiiii st, as my father used to say.

I walk towards the social worker, blocking mom's view, "You idiot. We finally got mom sold on the idea of assisted living after assuring her that where ever she'd go, her little dog, would follow." Chili begins to growl, "You know I have power of attorney. Couldn't you have talked to me outside of the room?"

Thank god the stroke knocked out mom's short term memory. Hopefully in five minutes she'll forget this Hallmark moment. But, it is seared into my memory. Can someone hold my hand though all this? Hers? No time for that!

This isn't mom's first encounter with cruelty in the form of a caregiver. When in the hospital with atrial fibrillation, her doctor performed a procedure to shock her heart back into the rhythm - side effect could be a stroke.

A couple of days after this, my cousin Geena's visiting, she calls me, "they're taking your mom for an MRI, she might have had a stroke." In the background I hear a medical professional questioning my mother, "When did this start? Their voice gets louder, "Why didn't you tell us?" Meekly, my mom: "my vision has been off for a couple of days, I thought my eyes would get better."

The hospital workers are pissed that my mom had a stroke and didn't tell them. They're blaming the victim! These so called caretakers are annoyed that a patient who has lost capacity for short term memory – even her own name—didn't remember to tell them something.

"Cinnamon, Cinnamon," spills from mom's mouth. My cousin asks me, "What does it mean?" In childhood we had a dog named Cinnamon, but that couldn't be it. Duh, I'm in mom's apartment sitting next to her cinnamon colored dog. What have I been telling you? It's all about the canine. Temporarily, the spice becomes a term of endearment. I never heard it myself, once the doctors decided to dismiss mom, they gave me four days to find a facility which would take her and the dog. My mother became a bystander in her own life.

To do list: Find pet friendly ALFs, locate all the hidden cash around the apartment. Do you know, I found $10,000 in the freezer? Literally, cold, hard cash. Right next to the gooey fudgesicles.

On the to do list: go to the bank, underneath - buy dog food.

Everything's on my list except - - visit mom. No time for that. Every time my phone rings and mom scrolls along the top of the screen. I think, God, what does she want now? Guilt takes hold as I push the ignore button, I feel like screaming: Mom, I'm sorry. You probably need hand-holding right now but if there's a chance in hell of getting you and your dog into an ALF in four days there's no time to take care of you.

In my imaginary conversation: Sorry, It's all about the canine, she needs to be walked and fed. You have nurses doing those things for you.

Meanwhile things keep getting added to the to do list: Get the death certificate of my step father's first wife, who died at least thirty years ago. Give away a car, titled in a dead man's name.

I meet with the administrators of my mom's housing complex, located across the street from the hospital. I can see her room from here but still no time to walk across the street to visit. Attempting to gather information regarding moving I ask for advice on ALFs. These women, laugh in my face, "Good luck finding a place that'll take a dog."

The big thing that keeps me up at night, isn't the powerlessness I feel with my mother's situation but the sadness for those who have no one to advocate for them. My mother has us, preserving her mementos, attempting to recreate this home in a new location. There was much evidence in the trash room at her complex that if there are no caretakers, keepsakes are pitched – wedding photos, hand embroidered pillows, family furniture. The permanently incapacitated patient is transferred to an unfamiliar terrain without a single familiar landmark.

If I was lucky enough to dream, the images would turn to, a leader of a revolution, a Care Crusader. Along with a cape, a pair of shears to cut through red tape, she has a sidekick, a little dog named Patience. I wake up with a jolt, still holding the to do list in one hand, my calming stone in the other. Maybe, if I squeeze it harder it will be more effective.

In between everything, my niece, Monique, her daughter, Daphne and I visit my father who recently fell and nearly died. We have noticed my Dad's crushing on my mom. They've been divorced for over thirty years, yet his blue eyes cloud over on the tough days and are sparkly on mom's good days. Dad's unaware but my stepmom; she notices.

My signature line during this time is, "I'm her P.O.A., here's her D.N.R. I have her advance directive too,"

In the middle of all this a text: Running someone else's life isn't for the faint of heart. Some days start off great and turn bad. Other's start horribly and even out. There's always a call to my Aunt Raquel. I'm hyperventilating as I tell her the challenges we've, "Now just calm down, let me think." she tells me. Sometimes she has an edge in her voice. Her tone's not as comforting as I'd like. But hell, Aunt Raquel's the same age as my mother. They've been friends since high school. Auntie's grieving the dramatic changes in her bestie while trying to do the best by me.

After touring four assisted living facilities with Monique and her mini-me, I settle on a crazy expensive place where the pooch will be pampered.

Monique, Daphne and I stop at Burger King, after lunch I'm going to sign on the dotted line. I have some anxiety; mom's lawyer emphasized three letters: P.O.A. You need those initials each time you sign for your mother otherwise your ass is on the line.

I call my cousin, "Is putting my mom in an ALF okay?" Her response, "You need to stop worrying about money. Who knows, your mother might not even live that long." I think she was trying to be positive.

That night, my niece, her baby, the dog and I are in my mother's apartment getting ready for the movers in the morning. "Ring, Ring, Ring," Monique hands me the phone while mouthing, "Sorry, I hit accept by mistake."

"Just tell me how much it costs!" her uncle yells. Me: I don't know.

Uncle: What do you mean, you don't know?

Me: There were so many numbers and pages, I just closed my eyes and signed. No matter which ALF, they screw you on the price.

Him: That's just irresponsible.

Me: You think this is easy? Get your ass out here!

I hit the red button.

Turning to my niece, "If we told mom the price, it would kill her will to live." My niece starts laughing.

Monique: You all yell the same. Pop-pop, my dad, Uncle, and now you. You start out all nice then -- Bam -- screaming. Damn.

Daphne: Damn!

Me: Oh, Shit we can't curse in front of the baby.

Daphne: Shit.

Monique and I start laughing so hard we're crying.

That night I ask god: Can you please help me dial my inner bitch back? He answered, "No, my child, your mother and Chili aren't in the ALF yet, Keep the attitude."

Kindergarten Graduation Memoir

by

LouAnn Blocker

"May the 18! May the 18!" I sang to the tune of "Silent Night" over and over, aloud when no one else was around, and in my head when they were. It was the first date of significance in my life, besides my birthday and Christmas. It was recorded right there on the calendar by the telephone. The teachers sent home papers with the date. I could actually read some of the words.

I was the first in my family to graduate kindergarten. It wasn't available in the public schools yet, and my parents only chose to pay for private church kindergarten for me, because I was both the last child left at home, and an insatiably curious one. My mother wanted me out of her hair for a few hours a day, so she could finally be alone.

The event was to be held at the Catholic Youth Organization auditorium. The day before, we all walked in pairs from the school to the auditorium. I did not know the neighborhood, because I had always been driven by Mama or another mother there each day. I was fascinated by the houses, older than the 50s rancher I lived in. They were varied, clapboard two-story foursquare, then a stone house with a little tower in front that reminded me of Rapunzel's, then a brick house like mine, but made of much thinner bricks, and with a huge round window in front. We walked past a few more of these places, all unique and strange to me, in the mix of shade and sunlight that fell on the sidewalk as we traveled.

We crossed Texas Avenue in a bunch for safety, the teachers watching us and scanning the road for approaching cars at the same time. The class walked up the cool concrete steps, shaded by the large red brick building with its white columns out front. Upon entering, I was so chilled by the air conditioning after the walk that I shivered. There was a smell of old varnish emitting from the auditorium, and new wax in the tiled lobby we stood in.

Everyone proceeded up the aisle of the auditorium and got themselves on stage. We practiced walking on the strip of masking tape that marked the way from our solid little wooden chairs to the front of the stage, the microphone on its stand and the teachers standing near it, waiting to practice handing out our diplomas. I knew this event would be as much a test as coloring inside the lines, tying my shoes, and holding it until potty breaks were.

I knew the words and choreography to "I'm a Little Teapot." I could say the Pledge and the Lord's Prayer the Catholic way I had learned that year, always nailing it by remembering to stop before 'for thine is the kingdom...' Some of the Protestant kids were marked by that phrase and even after they should have known better, they still made the telltale lowering of their teeth to make an 'F' sound, not say 'Amen.' They were judged by all the other kids for it, Catholic and Protestant alike, by a mysterious rubric we didn't understand but rigidly followed.

We practiced singing and reciting, and the big day finally arrived. It started with curlers. They were metal rods about three inches long, with holes throughout. The hair was rolled onto these rods. On the outside, two thin pins on a hinge could then be swung over to secure the roller to a snap on the other side. It was a poor design. The hinged pins had a habit of getting tangled in my hair as Mama rolled it up, and it hurt, but I liked the way the whole set felt as it dried. My head was heavier. The metal cooled as it touched wet hair, and chilled my neck or cheek as it touched them. I also loved the end result, but I dreaded the process of removing them.

Mama's patience for the tasks of her day had usually worn thin way before my hair was dry, and she seldom took the curlers out with the same care she used to place them. In her defense, it was tricky. If any hair got caught in the hinges, the curl wouldn't just fall like a released spring from a coil, but could pull, and I would flinch. The task then would be for me to hold still while she attempted to save the spiral by unwinding the trapped hair and smoothing it back into the mass. If that didn't work, she took the hair between her wet fingers, shaped it back into the mass, squirted a little Aqua Net on her hands and ran them over my head to calm the frizzies and errant hairs.

Recently I found a few photos of myself from that time, and mused at the difference between my natural and set hair. I wondered why Mama bothered with the whole ordeal. My regular hair fell in soft waves. It looked cute, if unformed. But formed was the rule. Il faut souffrir pour etre belle. Why be simply cute when you could be belle? That's the question, I suppose.

After my hair was done, it was time to get ready. I loved clothes, but in the excitement, I didn't even notice what I wore on graduation night. At age six I knew all my dresses: pink with peach and pear appliqués, white with blue smocking, yellow with two flounces edged in lace, white with vertical ruffles on the bodice.

Mama did the usual thing of inserting my feet into lace-topped ankle socks, then turning them down neatly and evenly. She fastened the tiny buckles of my black patent leather Mary

Janes. I held my arms over my head as she put me in a full slip with a net petticoat, then a dress over it. Then she buttoned it up the back. Though scratchy and restrictive, those frilly outfits with big skirts were my delight. I felt beautiful and powerful when I rested my hands on the poufy laps of my princess dresses. At church, their folds took up space around me, so I couldn't be crowded by my rowdy brothers as we sat in a row on the pew. My still, ladylike behavior, ankles crossed and sitting up straight, pleased everyone else, too.

When we arrived at the CYO, I was absorbed by the human scene. Some kids clung to their parents and didn't respond to our teacher, Mrs. Arsenault, who was shepherding the early arrivals up the side steps of the stage. I wasn't nervous at all.

All of us girls looked different, but the boys were transformed. Their hair was slicked down with VO-5. They wore long pants, dress shirts, and ties. I was intrigued by the boys, and jealous of the Catholic girls who were wearing their first communion dresses. They looked like little brides, pure and angelic.

Once we were stationed in the wings, I did begin to feel anxious. Yesterday, during our practice, the area had been illuminated by the filtered, greenish light coming down from transom windows on the long back wall. The stage equipment, boxes, ropes, and various odd items were interesting to look at and wonder about. Tonight, it was dark back there. The shapes loomed like threatening monsters in the dusty gloom. Fortunately, I got distracted by hearing the audience taking their seats, and by the excitement rippling through the class, as we all crowded together backstage.

The warm breathing and the slight odor of earthworms that even the cleanest child gives off comforted me. My jitters abated as I stood there among the other kids. I started paying attention to what was happening on this most important night. Everyone smelled like starched clothes and unfamiliar hair products. We knew we needed to be quiet, but petticoats crinkled, and shoes scuffed dully against the oak floorboards. My waistband itched, but I knew better than to scratch.

We walked out in two rows to recite and sing, then be seated in order, A-L's in front and M-Z's in back. One little scholar took the admonition to walk on the tape literally. He walked the line as if it were a tightrope, carefully and slowly placing one foot directly in front of the other with arms outstretched, and I could hear a few people laughing. His face was red and his posture defeated as he returned to his seat. Their laughter made me queasy. Would I make a mistake? Wasn't it wrong of big people to laugh?

I realized that night that I could be judged by others who wouldn't dare ever put themselves on a stage, and who relished the safety of the darkness.

"Still I am drawn to the past where donuts never came in a box, but from a warm kitchen made with loving, weathered hands."

Of Value

by

Dori Bash

Washboards are a dime a dozen in the antique stores. A handy necessity of the past, used weekly, if not more. I have two that belonged to my grandma Eva and great grandma Minnie. One a child size, with metal ridges and worn wood, telling me much was expected of children back then.

I'll hang the washboards in my new utility room, finally displaying them after years of tucking them behind a mattress or beside the dryer. Their value lies in memories: the touch of an ancestral hand wringing a soft, worn apron after kneading cardamom bread, or a quick pick in the hen house.

My grandparents' homes were uncluttered, large and luminous, spotlessly clean. One summer day, our station wagon rolled into the driveway to find great grandma Minnie with a dishpan of soapy water scrubbing the back door wooden steps. Who does that these days? No one I know. Perhaps they didn't have a hose.

Those six stairs were wide, at least five feet, and roughly hewn. Minnie in her late seventies, short and plump, her long, thin strands of gray hair wound up in a bun with two tortoise shell hairpins holding it loose, stood and waved, the stairs forgotten. All seven of us trampled up, unconcerned about the gravel and dust we left behind.

Coffee at the ready, the aroma so familiar. It meant cream and sugar in bone china cups, on saucers, and bites of yeasty, warm sugar breads. We grand-girls ran to the candy dishes placed just so on pretty doilies, lemon drops with sugar coating in one, melty mint flavors in the other. No need to ask permission, they were purposely filled for our visit.

Many times, I considered parting with the washboards. I dusted them off and fantasized what it might be like to use them to do the laundry, bending over a tub, with harsh lye soap, sore shoulders from the rinsing, the wringing, the hanging out to dry. The clothes quite dirty after a week of wearing, with mud and manure, dust and sweat.

The washboards are a connection to my past, where I come from. Hard working folk who knew how to make ends meet with a lot of do it your selfness. Where chickens were housed and fed, cleaned up after, to produce the precious eggs. Where berry patches were weeded, pruned and picked clean. Where cows were milked, cream skimmed, butter churned, to bake scrumptious biscuits, cookies, casseroles and puddings.

These days we push buttons to wash our clothes, clean our dishes and cook our food. I embrace the modern conveniences. Still, I am drawn to the past where donuts never came in a box, but from a warm kitchen made with loving, weathered hands.

I see the value now—now that it is too late to ask my questions and offer my gratitude for all their hard work, love and care. The washboards hang proudly in my laundry room and remind me to tell my stories to my children, my grandchildren and extended family to ensure we keep the legacy of our elders alive so we remember who we are and where we come from.

Value lives in the heart.

Prairie Dogs and Tunnels

by

Stevie Stephens Burden

CindyB and I have been friends for over 40 years and we have been camping together every single one of those years. Sometimes with a group of girlfriends and more recently just on our own. So when we hit the road to go camping in 2010, I had no idea it would end up being such an adventure. Over the course of 11 days, we drove 1100 miles into the southwest and back.

On this particular trip we were driving to Zion National Park, planning to visit the canyon floor and do a bit of hiking. Neither of us had ever been to Zion. I've always wanted to stand at the bottom of that canyon and look up. However, somehow we took a wrong turn on our way and that was the beginning of a great adventure.

We found ourselves on a two-lane highway that instead of going down into the bottom of the canyon was winding its way up a cliff face in a series of death-defying switchbacks. Cindy was driving and the dizzying heights and lack of a place to turn around were making her extremely uncomfortable. This was the second day into our trip and it was a construction nightmare. The already narrow two lanes went down to one as we approached a flagger at the bottom of a very steep hill. He waved us through hurriedly and so we had no choice but to keep going up. At the next switch back we saw a sign that said, to our utter dismay, "Tunnel – Next 7 miles" - SEVEN miles?

"Holy c*#p who builds a seven-mile-long tunnel in the first place - on the side of a cliff with no place to turn around and then closes one lane?"

I was appalled.

"Crazy ones," she replied in a slightly terrified whisper.

Then my worst nightmare began to unfold as Cindy turns to me and says, "I can't stop shaking – you have to drive...."

I don't like heights and I especially didn't like small curvy roads up a cliff but clearly I was going to have to step up and do it. CindyB was clearly not able to continue she was shaking so hard.

"Well okay but you'll find a place to pull off. There haven't been very many," my voice betraying me with a quiver.

Suddenly a perfect place to pull over materialized. Just my luck. Reluctantly I walked around the car and got into the driver's seat trying to put on a brave face as I buckled up. We brought up the rear and as I pulled out onto the road and into the tunnel. It looked like a great gaping maw across the road. It was magnificent and terrifying at the same time.

It took a minute for my eyes to adjust as we entered into the dusky tunnel. It was dark but not pitch-black.

"Can you see the light ahead?"

"Yeah it's weird," she replied in a quiet voice.

It revealed itself to be a carved window through the tunnel wall. The opposite wall filling the frame. I paused just long enough for Cindy to take a quick picture from the passenger's seat. We continued to move through this weird world of light and shadow with windows, in mouth gaping wonder. We had completely lost sight of the car ahead of us at some point. I realize now that was a mistake but it was such a bewitching world.

We were caught in the heart of this quiet when I realized that I could see light at the end of the tunnel up around the next curve. We were jerked firmly back into the real world as a big black pickup truck rolled beside us and from out of the dark we clearly heard a very big voice yelling from the cab, "HEY WHAT ARE YOU DOING IN HERE?"

I didn't have much time to contemplate as the black pick up rolled past, a very large bus in the middle of the road followed closely by a long line of cars stacked up behind it. I had forgotten it was a construction zone. The bus pulled to a stop in the middle of the road and squatted menacingly before us, lights shining in our eyes and dust settling around us. The door of the bus slowly swung open and out stepped two very large men in uniforms. They slowly approached our car.

I rolled my window down and a voice out of the dark slowly says, "I'm sorry ma'am but you can't go through."

"What do you mean we can't go through?"

"I'm really sorry but I can't move over to let you through. I'm too tall and there isn't enough clearance," and then the most dreaded words of all, "you're going to have to turn around and go back."

"But the end is right up there!"

"I know, but it's no good we can't back up," came the soft empathetic reply.

I finally managed to turn around. We pulled in behind the pilot car and slowly followed him back the way we had come, into the long winding darkness of the seven-mile tunnel. As we left the tunnel the pilot car motioned us around. We found ourselves being motioned to turn around and once again get in line to go back through the now familiar tunnel, all seven miles of it.

We finally got through all seven miles of that tunnel. Just past the end of the construction there was a large turn out and we both agreed we needed a break. We just needed a couple of minutes to adjust to the world of light again and switch drivers. CindyB stopped on her way around the car and pulled out her camera. "What are those animals?" she asked.

I looked over and recognized a prairie dog colony. They were, as prairie dogs do, standing up next to their holes with paws on their chests and watching our every move.

"They're prairie dogs," I told her as I watched them watch us.

"I feel like they're talking about us," she said as they chattered away.

"They probably are. I wonder what they're saying," I mused, "stupid woman got in big trouble...," we chuckled and pulled back onto the road looking ahead and wondering what the next corner would reveal.

Later that night as we sat safely tucked into our tent in Bryce Canyon National Park, CindyB pulled out a book about Native American beliefs and their relationship with animals and their spirits. Each animal is endowed with its own characteristics and purpose. Having grown up in Indian Country I understand and respect the teachings of my childhood and there is usually a message or lesson that I can learn contained in them. This would be no different.

Cindy sat quietly reading while I finished making up my bed. As I sat down on my bed across from her, running her finger down the table of contents she causally asked, "did you know that prairie dogs were one of the animals in this book?"

"I don't think I've ever read that one," I replied, "what's it say?"

She came to the end of the short passage on Prairie Dogs and stopped reading. She looked straight at me and said, "You are not going to believe what this says at the end."

"Why? What does it say?"

She looked back down at the book for a moment and then back up at me with a smile just catching on at the corners of her mouth, and began to read, "It says if prairie dog has come into your life today, he's trying to tell you to remember, that those tunnels run both ways...."

"No it doesn't!" I said incredulous, "Let me see it."

I couldn't believe it but there it was. A quote, that will echo in my brain for the rest of my life, "he's trying to tell you to remember that those tunnels run both ways..."

So, I have met the light at the end of the tunnel and it was in fact a bus. But never again will I automatically assume that even if the light at the end of the tunnel is a bus that it necessarily means all is lost. I know now that I will always have the freedom to change course if I so choose. And so it is with the rest of the worlds and people that inhabit this planet.

I will always have a choice to give another person's world the benefit of the doubt. I realize now that just because something is a popular belief that doesn't mean I have to go that direction too. I can choose to understand that the way I see my world and the perceptions of others can be different, even in conflict. I can still choose to give others and their worldviews respect and honor our differences instead of condemning what makes me different from them.

Salmon Cycle: Ethereal Passage

by

Kristin Koptiuch

Swirls of trapped salmon roil the slate gray water in the Nehalem River Hatchery,
Keeping just ahead of two ODFW* men wearing high bib waders.
The men slowly move hip-deep through the fish trap tank.
They're herding fish, by steadily combing forward a fence that spans the tank's width.
Cornered at tank's end, hundreds of squirming coho salmon become easy prey for the net.

After a dry summer on Oregon's north coast—a new normal wrought by climate change,
Mid-October rains have finally swelled rivers and streams.
The coho salmon endured their long salty ocean voyage of maturason, and finally
Flowing fresh waters released the fish from their extra-long wait in the brackish estuary.
Those coho that effectively evaded the flashy lures trolled by legions of Nehalem Bay fishermen Could now return to spawn in their natal streams.

Our tank-trapped coho had swum up the fish ladder from the Nehalem River's North Fork to the hatchery from whence they came—only to meet a dead end.
There'd be no spawning for most, save a few plump females
Whose eggs would be harvested for next year's hatchery brood.
A few wild coho somehow gone astray would be returned to the river For a second chance to find their proper upstream breeding waters.

A hapless fate awaits the other 300 salmon wriggling in their pen.

Scooped up by the dozen in a rectangular net now rested on deck hooks just above water, The netted salmons' frenzied writhing gradually subsides.

An ODFW handler seizes each fish in turn and calls out its classification
While a hatchery record-keeper in white coveralls jots down the tally:
HATCHERY MALE, HATCHERY FEMALE, WILD MALE, WILD FEMALE,
or JACK, the smaller immature males that return from the ocean too soon.

Each fish next gets unceremoniously stunned by a whack to the head with a baseball bat,
And is passed up to our team of volunteer salmon harvesters from Smiley Brothers and Sisters.* Two of us take turns wrangling with gloved hands each still-wriggling coho,
Cradling them over to a bloodied cutting table where two more volunteers slit the fish's gills to bleed them out.
Dead for certain now, coho bodies get piled together in huge food grade plastic fish totes.

It takes quite a while to process 300 salmon.
The netting. The writhing. The stunning. The pass. The gill cutting. The binning. Repeat.
I feel a confounding thrill as I hold each magnificent fish squirming at its life's end.
The netting. The writhing. The stunning. The pass. The gill cutting. The binning. Repeat.
I am discomfited too, to play my minor role in the doomed fate of so many salmon.
The netting. The writhing. The stunning. The pass. The gill cutting. The binning. Repeat.
Working together, our team fills two industrial totes to their brims with bloodied coho.
Three hundred repeats take upon me an affective toll that words alone cannot atone.

The salmon will move on, a harvest destined for an afterlife voyage through the food chain, To be cleaned, filleted, the large ones cut, canned, and labelled, the jack fillets flash frozen, Ultimately to the delight of patrons of area food pantries and senior meals programs.

I cannot move on. I can't shake that day's poignancy.
Cradling more salmon than I could likely catch in a lifetime if I were a fisherman,
My arms ferried unbidden hundreds of Oregonians' sacred fish across ethereal realms:
From the living to the dead, from the wild to the human food chain.

*Notes: ODFW is the Oregon Department of Fish and Wildlife. The Smiley Brothers and Sisters coho salmon harvest also partners with Tillamook Bay Seafood and Bell Buoy to process and can the fish; Neah Kah Nie High School art students design the labels each year. Thousands of cans of salmon go to area food pantries, and fillets of the smaller immature jack salmon delight residents of local assisted living facilities and senior meal recipients. The grand total was 653 salmon for the Smiley Salmon Harvest in 2023.

Two Pans

by

Anndell Thompson

Sheep once grazed the meadows of the Lostine River Canyon. The ascent was dangerous for shepherds and sheep. Flocks were driven up the canyon from Wallowa Valley. Steep canyon walls meant narrow trails and loose rock. Shepherds camped near the Lostine River falls, the source of the Lostine River. The meadows are lush in the canyon, perfect for the sheep. There were nails in the red-barked pines where they hung their cooking pans. The pans were left on the trees until they were needed the next year.

The name "Two Pans" has been used for over a century. Now there is an Oregon State Horse Camp there called Two Pans. I stay there whenever I find the time, with my horse "Mo." Life here is peaceful, yet it can be exciting. Storms, wild animals, narrow trails above the canyon, uninformed hikers, all add to the variety. Still, there is constancy. Peace and contentment win out overall.

I named my horse Mo, since he turned out to be "more" than I bargained for. We met at an auction. No one bid on him, which served me perfectly. No one bid on me either, so we were a perfect pair. We were young, newly acquainted, as we sought each other's depth. He was only halter-broken. I started his training slowly, gently. As much for his safety as mine. Mo was big, seventeen hands. I decided he was part thoroughbred and the other half cow pony. Ideal. Finally, we felt ready for the arena. We started traveling from one dusty rodeo to the next. We tried calf roping. I cannot say which one of us was the worst. He charged into the arena like a scared rabbit, forgetting why we were there. I was no better—especially the scared rabbit part.

A silent trust developed between us. When my balance was off, he would move over under me. Working together, slowly, over time, respect grew to companionship. Still, the

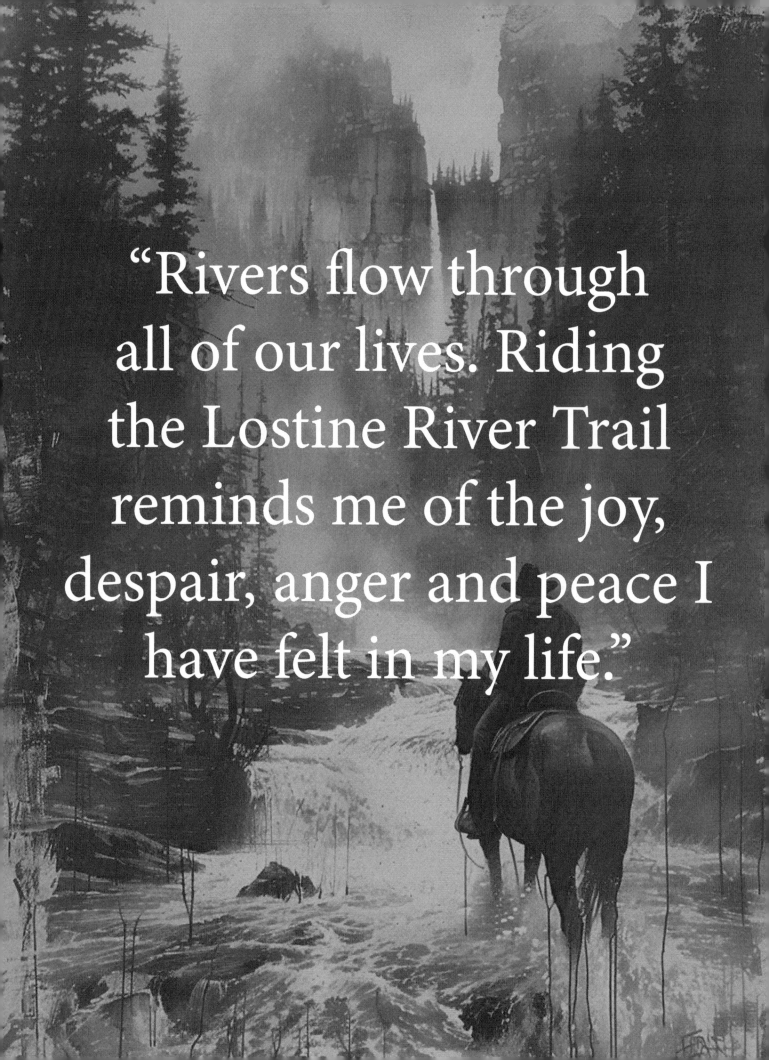

"Rivers flow through all of our lives. Riding the Lostine River Trail reminds me of the joy, despair, anger and peace I have felt in my life."

years wore us down, and we began to feel frayed at the seams. Not physically, mentally. We both felt it. No definite reason, we just needed some stillness. I sold everything and we moved near Two Pans.

All trails follow rivers when you live in a canyon. What a magnificent river the Lostine is. Each step brings a fresh connection with nature. My saddle creaks, softly, following the motion of Mo's wither's. Ancient Ponderosa Pines form a canopy above us. Still in snow, the mountains reflect a rosy glow as the sun breaks over the canyon walls. The river runs silent and deep here. Dragonflies dart over the still surface. Green banks gently caress the river, as a familiar lover.

The roar of a waterfall deepens the river's voice. Steep canyon walls echo the fury. Fine mist drifts upwards, droplets of ice from above the timberline. Mo picks his way through boulders and scree with ease. He is sure-footed, despite his age, even at five-thousand feet. Once he did lose his footing, and he just sat down. We slid to the bottom unharmed. I step down below the falls, and Mo fondles the sweet water. As I swing into the saddle, a pine squirrel chatters its discomfort at our intrusion.

The river widens. Rippling water embraces a hundred thousand pebbles, reflected in twinkling prisms of light. Impulsively, I turn Mo across the shallow stream bed. As we splash our way to opposite bank, Mo nods his head to show his approval, cantering across the meadow. A doe hurries her fawn into cover. Dismounting, I slip Mo's bridle. I snooze, listening to the sound of Mo enjoying lunch.

Further down the trail there is a fly fisherman working the river. There are boulders, rocks, and runs where the rainbows hide. The angler's crumpled hat boasts a collection of feathered flies. He is booted almost head to toe. Standing in the swiftest current, he seems part of the river. Standing with knees flexed, he calmly awaits the anticipated strike. The stubble of a beard glistens white in the sunlight. His brief escape from the rigors of civilization. He gazes steadily into the rippling water flowing around him, not noticing his glasses have slipped down on his nose. It is not what you see; it is what you expect to see. Each cast flies in graceful loops, kissing the water. Suddenly, a trout leaps wildly, prey to man's trickery. In a splashing panic, it runs upstream, leaping into the air, trying to throw the hook. Loosening the drag on his reel, the fisherman allows the trout to believe it is free. Hiding behind a rock, it trusts that it has found safety. But the line has been skillfully reeled in as the trout swam. Now, the rainbow is tiring, finding he is unable to fight the constant pressure on its jaw. Yet, the fish begins its struggle anew, leaping in the air, flashing its rainbow. Nature's struggle to survive is concentrated in its frantic action.

Slowly reeling in his prize and taking his net from his belt, he slips it beneath the firm belly of the rainbow. Probing carefully for the barb-less hook, he removes the offensive bit of wire. The Rainbow, released, is wiser, but unharmed. The fisherman turns toward the riverbank, and first notices his silent audience. I nod hello from the saddle, complementing his sportsmanship. His wide whiskered grin bears witness that a battle is sometimes best when lost.

Rivers flow through all of our lives. Riding the Lostine River Trail reminds me of the joy, despair, anger, and peace I have felt in my life.

There were cool, deep, quiet pools. There were rapids that could have drowned me. There were thundering waterfalls that stifled my reason. I have learned to float my troubles away in the streams. Streams flow into rivers. Rivers rush to the sea.

My troubles go out with the tide. I only remember the quiet meadows.

Yaeki-san

by

Janine Iwaya

In the late eighties, when our house was brand new, my husband Teruo and I couldn't believe our luck in finding such a place. It was modern, with light flooding through several tall windows. The surrounding woods included two maple trees, big even then. One grew near each end of the narrow back deck, a deck which ran the width of the house. Huge firs stood at various spots uphill, in front of the house. The shade they provided was a cool change from the mid-summer heat Teruo's mother, Yaeki, had left behind when she arrived for her first visit from Japan. She was surprised to find us living in such a large place.

"Five families would fit in this house," Teruo laughed, translating his mother's comment for me. And added, "Japanese families."

He was proud of having a home to show his mother. I quickly came to realize that Yaeki felt our house was evidence of her son's hard work. It was. It had taken almost seven years, really since Teruo and I had first married, to be able to afford it. Like many who'd been raised in post war Japan, he thought owning a home was unimaginable.

His work as a commercial photographer had made it possible.

Teruo had grown up in Tokyo with his older sister Takeko, where life had been difficult for them after Yaeki divorced their father. The war had ended a year before he was born, but it was several years until she found permanent work at a factory.

Two weeks after my mother-in-law arrived, it was decided she'd stay alone in the house one night while Teruo and I attended a friend's wedding. It had been a mistake. Returning late the next day, we found his mother with a badly swollen eye, possibly from a wasp sting. She'd been pulling weeds in our wild backyard.

"When I reluctantly admitted feeling at a loss, being on my own with my mother-in-law, he reminded me again to learn Japanese 'if I really wanted to communicate with his mother.'"

"What if it had been worse?" Teruo said, mad at himself. "How could she have gotten help?" I rummaged through the bathroom drawer for something to numb Yaeki's pain as she turned away, hiding her swollen eye. "She's ashamed and embarrassed at seeing how shocked we are," he said.

The next morning as we ate breakfast together, I said, "Please tell your mother it isn't necessary to work in the yard or clean the floors in the house, like she does every day."

"She only wants to feel she's contributing somehow," was Teruo's sharp replied. I felt misunderstood.

For the next two weeks Yaeki spent hours with her son at his studio; they'd often depart before I was up for work. And she'd sometimes join him on location. "We were shooting in the Park Blocks today," Teruo said as we ate dinner one night. "Mom enjoyed watching all of us at work, and the crew got a kick out of seeing her."

He would talk about their day as the three of us sat together for dinner; Teruo at the head of the table, translating questions I had and the comments Yaeki made. But she often just listened quietly as we talked, not understanding what was said.

The next week he took his mother to Seattle. The train ride was something new for both of them. Visiting the big city with its corporate headquarters gave her a chance to see where her son did much of his fashion catalog work. And she got to meet the art directors and stylists he worked with.

Another day that July I listened at the table as Teruo described how much fun they'd had on their drive to the coast and back. "It was her first look at the Pacific Ocean," he said, smiling, "at least from this side. And she loved riding in my MG."

I worked full-time that summer and missed being part of their trips. But seeing them talk and laugh as we ate dinner, made me realize how much it meant to them to be together; for Yaeki to see how things had turned out for her son.

I thought of the first five years Teruo spent in Oregon, attending college and never once calling home. Yaeki paid his expenses those years and the price of a phone call was just too much to spend. Ten years had passed since college but now she had seen where he'd spent those years and the time since.

During Yaeki's first summer visit, Teruo was sometimes out of town for work. When I reluctantly admitted feeling at a loss, being on my own with my mother-in-law, he reminded me again to learn Japanese "if I really wanted to communicate with his mother."

"I'll work on it," I said. "I'll work on it."

On the nights alone with Yaeki, I'd prepare dinner after work, and we'd sit and eat together. I had decided to try and make conversation, using the few Japanese words I knew.

"O-shi desu-ka?" I asked, smiling at Yaeki-san while hoping the question I'd asked had been 'How is it?' I recalled delicious was a word she had been practicing. I wondered if she'd use it.

Pausing to look at the list of words her son had urged her to learn, she quickly replied, "Delicious. Yes." We laughed together. And I stumbled through another phrase in my limited Japanese. But for the most part Yaeki ate with her eyes down. As I talked, she'd glance, smiling, and look briefly in my direction, as if she recognized an English word she'd learned or somehow understood my attempt at Japanese. More often though, Yaeki had no response. I decided she didn't understand me. Or perhaps she didn't know the English reply, I thought. In the end, we would sit and finish eating in silence.

With dinner over I'd nervously anticipate the long evening ahead, sitting on the back deck, side by side in our canvas chairs. On that first visit, especially, I had tried to make conversation as we sat watching the evening sky. "O tenki atsui desu, hi?" I said, asking Yaeki if she agreed that the weather was hot.

"Yes," Yaeki replied. "Hot." She'd stretched the word out in an effort to get it right. We laughed together, again. But talk would eventually slow as I grew tired of the effort it took, and we'd end the evening quietly watching the sky turn from twilight to dark.

Of all the visits to see us, that early one was Yaeki's best, when everything her son shared about his life in the U.S. was new to her. After several more summer trips, she made what turned out to be her final and longest visit, staying almost three months.

Much of her time that trip, Yaeki spent taking long walks and was gone for hours. I had quit my job by then and was often at home.

One evening just after Teruo got back from work and Yaeki was resting downstairs in her room, I mentioned to him how worried I was at his mom's habit of being gone most of the day. He said only, "She likes wandering through the nearby arboretum, and around the woods near the zoo. It's her way of making less work for you, by not being underfoot." He turned to look at me and said, "My mother just feels it's better to be out for the day. She doesn't want to bother you for food when she's hungry, and doesn't feel she should open the cupboards, as if she had the run of the house. Besides, she likes picking blackberries to bring back and share, and she enjoys her time in the park, out of the way.

It hurt to hear how she felt. We had never been able to talk. In that moment I regretted having missed so many opportunities to do so, never having learn Japanese.

"But what does she eat and drink, out there alone all day?" I asked. "She must get thirsty.

"She fills up on blackberries," Teruo replied. "I gave her money last week to get something to drink from the ice cream vendor near the zoo." Teruo seemed amused, saying, Mom couldn't understand why he wouldn't take her money and give her a bottle of water. When I asked her how much the sign said it cost, I realized I hadn't given her enough."

"He should have just given her the water," I replied. I recognized his shameful behavior.

Yaeki and I had been alone one night, early in that last visit, when she found me in the kitchen, after our meal together. She beckoned me to the back deck. I ignored her, acting as if I didn't understand her gesture, inviting me to admire the beautiful pink sunset.

She turned and walked back to the deck and sat, alone, watching until the light was gone.

JOIN US NEXT YEAR FOR OUR

2025
ROCKAWAY WRITERS RENDEZVOUS

VISIT RBWRITERS.COM FOR DETAILS

Made in the USA
Middletown, DE
14 May 2024

54217259R00097